MERILYN COPLAND PH

HE WALKED WITH US

A GEOGRAPHICAL DEVOTIONAL GUIDE TO THE LAND OF ISRAEL

CONTENTS

INTRODUCTION

AND ACKNOWLEDGMENTS

Sometimes the most significant things in life sneak up on us.

My first trip to Israel was one surprising moment after the other. I joined a tour that was already planned and headed to Israel. The funds were provided for me to go, so I packed up and went, not sure of what to expect. Sure, I had studied the Bible before — even memorized hundreds of site names and locations throughout the land of Israel — but I never imagined my life would be changed so dramatically.

As our bus pulled up to each site, I began see the hand of God in a way I never had before. As we studied the Bible stories in the places they happened, I gained new level of biblical understanding and my relationship with God was impacted forever.

There is something unexplainable about this land. Even if we wrote volumes about Israel, it isn't until you see it for yourself that you can appreciate just how special this small country is to God's story. I have a firm belief that God has preserved this land, not just for a place to fulfill future prophecy, but to bring His children on earth into a closer relationship with Himself. Just as any good preacher will use sermon props or stories, so God uses the land of Israel as a visual aid to bring to life the lessons of the past and the applications for the present.

I can't think of a better way for you to spend your time and money than to study Israel and to see this amazing place for yourself. While it is always good to learn and become educated, gaining greater head knowledge cannot be the mere purpose of studying or visiting Israel. This land stands as a monument to a living God. Israel should bring you closer to Him rather than cause you to be distracted by fascinating findings, significant rocks or sacred site. Whether you are a minister or a mechanic, a mom or a medical expert, the call to know God is woven throughout the fabric of our life. Israel has an open invitation for all to come and grow closer with God and bear witness to His goodness through all generations (Psalm 100:5).

This book is a journey more than a project. It has taken countless hours to complete this third edition, or should I say, the first leg of the journey. However, with each passing mile marker I was blessed to have great friends on the voyage with me.

First and foremost, thank you Merilyn Copland for taking my call and being so willing to dream with me, without even knowing me. Your expertise in the archeology of Israel has made this book an excellent resource.

My prayer is that we will be partners for a very long time and bring the life changing history of Israel to the life application of modern believers.

Thank you, Lisa Moore, for the passion you have for the modern and ancient Israel. You are one of the loudest voices that God has used to speak to me about my calling to serve the people of Israel and take believers there to be changed by the truth of the Bible. I love your family! I trust God will continue to use you in mighty ways; He already has in my life. I look forward to having you and Michael as my co-leaders for "West Bank Tours by Weidmann."

Guy. You are more than a guide; you are a true friend. You have taught me more about the Bible than just about anyone in my life – thank you! It is my sincere hope that we grow old together as we lead people through that special land. Hopefully we will be 80-year-old men still climbing rocks and paths telling stories and seeing lives transformed. Thanks for your friendship.

And most dear to my heart - my wife, Molly, and my family. You have supported all of my crazy dreams. You allowed me travel to Israel while you were pregnant (twice). I loved that some of Gracie's first words were "Israel" and "Jerusalem." You are an amazing wife. Thank you for letting me go to Israel to become a better man, husband, dad, pastor and believer. I can't wait to take you there – that will be a dream come true! I love you.

And here's to you – my reader and companion on an Israel tour. Thank you for trusting Merilyn and I to teach you through this written word. If we are on a tour together, then thank you also for trusting me with your time and money to experience God and the truth of the Bible in away that can only happen by going there.

This has been a wonderful journey, and I believe it is only the beginning.

Josh Weidmann.

Josh Weidmann
March 2014

GEOGRAPHICAL
AREAS OF THE HOLY LAND

UPPER GALILEE & GOLAN HEIGHTS ———————

GALILEE REGION ————————————

COASTAL PLAIN ————————————

LOWER GALILEE & JEZREEL VALLEY ——————

SHEPHELAH ——————————————

HILL COUNTRY OF JUDEA & SAMARIA —————

JERUSALEM ——————————————

DEAD SEA, WILDERNESS & NEGEV ——————

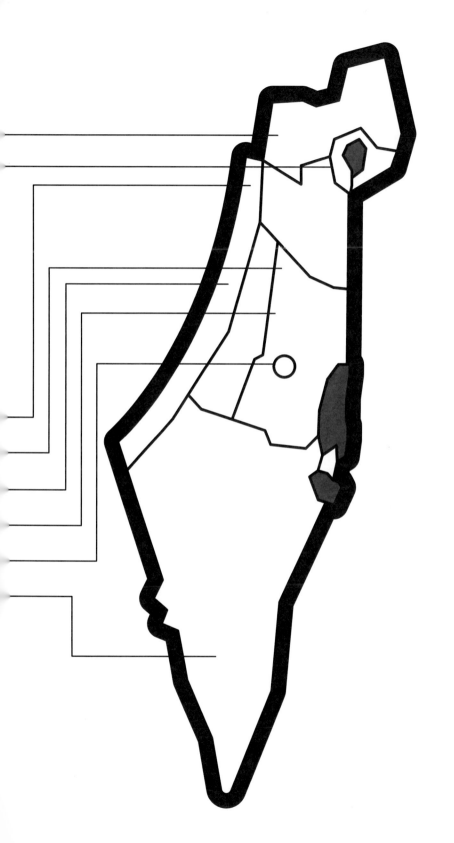

MOUNT HERMON

THE MOUNTAINS THAT DECLARES
HIS MAJESTY

Tabor and Hermon sing for joy at your name!

BACKGROUND, ARCHAEOLOGY, AND SIGNIFICANCE

This lofty mountain, stretching for a distance of 30 miles, has several peaks. From a distance, it looks more like a mountain range than a single mountain. The highest point is on the southwest side and most visible on the approach from the Sea of Galilee.

The fertile fields below Hermon set off the white, snow-capped peaks. Skiers enjoy these slopes in the winter and spring with lifts and facilities at Newe Ativ. The lower slopes of the mountain are known for orchards of apple, plum, cherry, pear, almond, and a forest of pine.

The summit of Mount Hermon rises to an elevation of over 9,200 feet, dominating the landscape of northern Israel. The limestone mountain has steep slopes on its eastern side, but the stepped terraces on its western side receive more dew, rain, and snow.

The ground water from Mount Hermon and the runoff from the melting snow form the headwaters of the Jordan River. Historically, this lush area was teeming with wildlife:

> *Come with me from Lebanon, my bride,*
> *come with me from Lebanon. Descend*
> *from the crest of Amana, from the top of*
> *Senir, the summit of Hermon, from the*
> *lions' dens and the mountain haunts of*
> *the leopards.*
>
> SONG OF SOLOMON 4:8

From the summit of Mount Hermon on a clear day, the view to the south includes the mountains of Gilead, the Huleh Valley, the Sea of Galilee, and the Jordan Valley beyond. When looking toward the east, you can see the plain extending all the way to Damascus. The view toward the

REFERENCES

Deuteronomy 3:8–9; 4:48
Joshua 11:3, 17; 12:1, 5; 13:5
1 Chronicles 5:23
Psalm 42:6; 89:12; 133:3
Song of Solomon 4:8
Ezekiel 27:5 (Senir)

west includes the mountains of Upper Galilee, Mount Carmel, the Mediterranean coast, and the mountains of Lebanon. Looking north from the peak, the rest of the Eastern Lebanon mountain range fills the skyline.

MOUNT HERMON IN HISTORY

Mount Hermon was considered the northern border of the territory conquered by Joshua. It was allotted to half of the tribe of Manasseh (1 Chronicles 5:23), but the history of the mountain goes back much farther. The Egyptians knew it as Sirion. The Amorites, as well as later Assyrian conquerors, called it Mount Senir (Ezekiel 27:5). The name Mount Hermon comes from the Hebrew root word meaning "taboo" or "consecrated." Archaeologists have found numerous cultic areas attesting to the religious use of the mountain throughout the first millennium B.C..

In the second century B.C., an Arab tribe, known as the Itureans, migrated into the Huleh Valley and onto the slopes of Mount Hermon. When the area came under Roman control, Mark Antony gave the area to Cleopatra as a gift. After the death of the ill-fated couple, Caesar Augustus gave the land to Herod the Great, with the responsibility of clearing the area of bandits who preyed on travelers. The defeated Itureans, who had used the natural strongholds of the mountain slopes as hideaways, were recruited into the Roman army. They had an excellent reputation as archers.

THE ARCHAEOLOGY OF MOUNT HERMON

Mount Hermon was considered a sacred place by several groups of people over the centuries. Archaeologists have surveyed more than twenty temples and sacred enclosures on the mountain. Many of the sites appear to be Canaanite or Phoenician cult centers dedicated to Baal.

Later, in the two centuries before Christ, niches and grottos were cut into the rock at these sacred areas, not unlike the ones you see at Caesarea Philippi. Beginning in the first century A.D., temples were built in a Greco-Roman style, even though the people worshiping there were Itureans.

MOUNT HERMON IN THE BIBLE

In the Old Testament, Mount Hermon formed a natural barrier between Israel and Syria. The area around Mount Hermon belonged to the half-tribe of Manasseh, who lived east of the Jordan River. Although no significant events in the Old Testament are recorded to have happened here, it is mentioned for its abundant water, wood, and wildlife.

Herod the Great controlled the area around Mount Hermon in the New Testament era until his death in 4 B.C., and then ownership was passed to his son Herod Philip II (Luke 3:1).

Some scholars believe that Mount Hermon is a possible location for Christ's transfiguration. The main basis for this assumption is that the context of the event, given in Matthew 16:13 and 17:1, is near Caesarea Philippi. If the transfiguration did happen in the same area, then the nearest "high mountain" is Mount Hermon. The other possible location is Mount Tabor, which is a two-day walk from the base of Mount Hermon.

During the transfiguration, Jesus' garments became radiant before the very eyes of Peter, James, and John. Moses and Elijah appeared with Jesus. A voice came out of a bright cloud saying, "This is My Son, whom I love; with Him I am well pleased. Listen to Him!" (Matthew 17:5). The disciples fell at Jesus' feet terrified. When they looked up, they saw only Jesus.

SO WHAT CAN WE LEARN FROM MOUNT HERMON?

Behold, how good and pleasant it is when brothers dwell in unity!
It is like the precious oil on the head, running down on the beard, on
the beard of Aaron, running down on the collar of his robes! It is like
the dew of Hermon, which falls on the mountains of Zion!
For there the Lord has commanded the blessing, life forevermore.

PSALM 133

Lofty Mount Hermon, towering more than 9,000 feet above sea level, is beautiful with its year-round snow-capped peaks. Without Mount Hermon, Israel would be a desert wasteland. Nearly all the water in the country comes from this mountain. Moisture blowing in from the Mediterranean Sea forms clouds around this towering peak, causing rain and snow to fall upon Northern Israel. The resulting precipitation, as well as runoff from the mountain itself, is the source of water for the Sea of Galilee and the Jordan River.

Meanwhile, Jerusalem and its surrounding hills farther south are on the edge of the desert. They depend on local rain showers for water. However, what if the abundant waters of Mount Hermon in the north could somehow be poured out on Jerusalem? Psalm 133 envisions a fantastic scene of the moisture of Mount Hermon falling directly on the mountains around Jerusalem. If this were possible, the mountains of Zion would see growth, and the unproductive desert would be transformed into fertile farmland.

According to the psalmist, this picture of unimaginable blessing reflects what it would be like if brothers could live together in unity. The benefits of unity would be poured out upon the people of God transforming their lives from a meager spiritual existence to lives of great blessing.

How sincere are we in our desire for harmony with others? When there is unity among people, the blessing of God comes to the world (John 17:20-26). Just as this majestic mountain gives life to the land of Israel, so our pursuit of peace among men blesses the world and gives the love of Christ to those who desperately need it. Jesus prayed for the blessings of unity to be poured out upon His people, on His disciples, and on all believers:

> *"I do not ask for these only, but also for those who will believe in Me through their word, that they may all be one, just as You, Father, are in Me, and I in You, that they also may be in us, so that the world may believe that You have sent Me. The glory that You have given Me I have given to them, that they may be one even as we are One, I in them and You in Me, that they may become perfectly one, so that the world may know that You sent Me and loved them even as You loved Me."*

JOHN 17:20–23, ESV

CAESAREA PHILIPPI

JESUS IS NOT JUST ANOTHER GOD

"Who do you say I am?"

MATTHEW 16:15

BACKGROUND, ARCHAEOLOGY, AND SIGNIFICANCE

BACKGROUND

Near the city of Dan is another place filled with beautiful ponds and woods. This area is fed by the Banias (the Arabic pronunciation of Paneas), a different tributary of the Jordan River. This gem is set against the cliffs of Mount Hermon. In ancient times, the large rock-hewn cave and nearby niches contained statues of Pan, the Greek god of flocks and shepherds. Excavations near the cave have revealed foundations of large buildings—possibly a temple to Augustus Caesar. Archaeologists also excavated an area to the right of the road that was used to enter the pools and caves of Panias or Caesarea Philippi, as it was known in the time of Christ.

THE HISTORY OF CAESAREA PHILIPPI

This site had probably been an area of sacred shrines long before the Greeks arrived and named it Paneas. The Greeks named the city after their god Pan. It was the Greek settlers in the area who set up a statue of Pan in the large grotto.

It was at Panias that a decisive battle had a profound effect on Jewish life. Judea was ruled by the Ptolemies, descendants of Alexander's general Ptolemy I, from their capital at Alexandria, Egypt for the first 125 years after the death of Alexander the Great. Their rule allowed a considerable amount of autonomy and complete religious freedom.

In 198 B.C., the army of the Ptolemies was defeated at Panias by the Seleucid army from Syria. The Seleucids began an oppressive rule over Israel from Antioch. Their ban on the practice of the Jewish religion eventually sparked the Mac-

QUICK FACTS

The city was earlier named Panias after the Greek god Pan who was believed to strike fear in his followers (the term "panic" is derived from Pan).

Herod Philip II renamed the city in honor of Caesar Augustus and himself.

Caesara Philippi was the home of numerous pagan shrines and temples throughout history.

In this area, Jesus asked his disciples, "Who do you say that I am?"

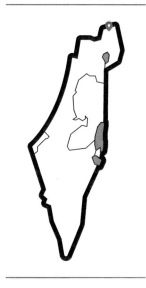

REFERENCES

Matthew 16:13–20

Mark 8:27–30

Luke 9:18–22

cabean revolt in 167 B.C., a revolt which resulted in a brief period of Jewish independence.

When Palestine later came under Roman rule in 20 B.C., Augustus added the area of northern Israel to the lands already controlled by Herod the Great. In gratitude, Herod the Great built a marble temple in Panias to honor Augustus.

After Herod's death in 4 B.C., his son, Phillip II (also known as Philip the Tetrarch), was confirmed by Caesar Augustus as ruler over the northeastern part of his father's kingdom. Taking a cue from his father, he established a new city here and renamed it after Caesar and himself.

CAESAREA PHILIPPI

Upon Philip's death in 34 A.D., his territory reverted to direct Roman control under the emperor Tiberias. Tiberias' successor Caligula eventually gave the area back to the Herodian family. In 60 A.D., Herod Agrippa renamed the city to Neronias, showing his loyalty to the Roman emperor Nero. During the reign of Nero, thousands of Jewish prisoners of war were killed in gladiatorial shows.

The city continued well into the Byzantine period with a mixture of Jewish and Christian populations. A Christian basilica was built in Caesarea Philippi in the fourth century. At the same time, however, the grotto remained in use as a pagan sanctuary with rituals sometimes involving human sacrifice. In the tenth or eleventh century A.D., a synagogue was built at the site. By the thirteenth century, the building had been converted into a mosque indicating that the Jewish population was gone.

CAESAREA PHILIPPI IN THE NEW TESTAMENT

After feeding the 4,000 and warning against the teaching of the Pharisees and Sadducees, Jesus traveled northward to Caesarea Philippi, the capital city of Herod Philip. The best that we know, this is as far north as Jesus ever traveled. Along the way, Jesus had an important conversation with His disciples.

When Jesus came to the region of Caesarea Philippi, He asked His disciples, "Who do people say the Son of Man is?" They replied, "Some say John the Baptist; others say Elijah; and still others, Jeremiah or one of the prophets." "But what about you?" He asked. "Who do you

say I am?" Simon Peter answered, "You are the Christ, the Son of the
Living God."

MATTHEW 16:13–16

It was at Caesarea Philippi that the disciples understood Jesus' true identity. This was the first place He revealed to His disciples that His mission was to go to Jerusalem, suffer, be killed, and rise again on the third day. This week-long lesson was capped by an event witnessed only by Peter, James, and John: the transfiguration.

It was here that Jesus put together for His disciples the twin truths of His humility and His glory. Some believe His transfiguration may have happened at Mount Hermon. Others believe it is more likely it happened on or around Mount Tabor, further south. Nonetheless, the question of Jesus' identity and the transfiguration happening soon thereafter was important for the disciples to see Jesus as truly divine.

THE ARCHAEOLOGY OF CAESAREA PHILIPPI

Excavations of Caesarea Philippi have concentrated in three areas: the cultic area near the cliffs of Mount Hermon, the public and administrative area, and the residential area to the west and south. In 1977, in the area southwest of the large cave, archaeologists found building blocks in a style characteristic of Herod the Great's building projects.

As excavators uncovered these building blocks, they were able to tell that it was a base standing nine feet above street level. It most likely the remains of the temple to Augustus erected by Herod the Great, which was decorated in marble. It appears the temple stood about 75 feet by 48 feet. A coin of Philip depicts this temple with four columns in front, but these columns have not been found.

In the center of the city, archaeologists have found public buildings arranged on terraces with roads going east and west. There is one monumental building with two lower stories that's remarkably well preserved. The building is almost 400 feet wide and consists of halls, fountains, vaulted underground passages, circular rooms, porticoes, and water channels. The twelve arches supporting the building can be seen from the road leading to the religious area. The use of the building may have been an Aesklepion, or sanctuary to the god of healing, the ancient equivalent of a medical center.

WHAT CAN WE LEARN FROM CAESAREA PHILIPPI?

The Greeks, after Alexander the Great, began an ambitious project of planting Greek cities throughout the area to unite their territories in one culture, language, and religion. In the north, the polytheistic Greeks and Syrians lived in great religious darkness. The Jews, an oppressed religious minority, lived in gloom.

In this region of Galilee near Mount Hermon, Jewish hopes and expectations ran high for the coming of the Messiah, and with Him, the arrival of the age to come.

> *Nevertheless, there will be no more gloom for those who were in*
> *distress. In the past He humbled the land of Zebulun and the land of*
> *Naphtali, but in the future He will honor Galilee of the Gentiles, by*
> *the way of the sea, along the Jordan. The people walking in darkness*
> *have seen a great Light; on those living in the land of the shadow of*
> *death a Light has dawned. You have enlarged the nation and increased*
> *their joy; they rejoice before You as people rejoice at the harvest, as men*
> *rejoice when dividing the plunder.*
>
> ISAIAH 9:1-3

One can imagine Jesus and His disciples walking toward the town shaking their heads. On the right was the glistening palace of Herod Philip and Salome, the woman who had asked for the head of John the Baptist on a platter. To the left was the great cave of Pan. Against the background of the red cliffs was the shining white Temple of Augustus.

These architectural wonders were built on land that was once called the Promised Land. With the worship of Pan and the rest of the Greek deities, it must have seemed as if the foreign gods had silenced the God of Israel. Elijah beat the prophets of Baal on Mount Carmel long ago, but now, there was no one to take on the gods of Greece and Rome that were worshiped at the foot of Mount Hermon.

> *"Who do people say that I am?"*
>
> MATTHEW 16:13

With this question, Jesus of Nazareth challenged those false gods. Peter answered, "The Son of the living God." Emperor Augustus, to whom the nearby temple was dedicated, was dead. Their gods were dead, but Jesus was the living God. Perhaps, there was hope after all.

The disciples had much to learn about what that meant. The Roman gods came to rule. The Messiah came to serve. The Greek gods came in strength. Jesus came as a baby in a manger. Caesar Augustus had made many suffer. The Lord of All would suffer for the sins of the world.

Perhaps, the disciples dreamed Jesus would win military victories. These visions were shattered as Jesus told what it meant to be Messiah. He was on an anointed mission to suffer and die. Peter was appalled. Jesus' words were in conflict with everything Peter believed the Messiah would do. He expected Jesus to receive popular acclaim as Deliverer.

> *From that time on Jesus began to explain to His disciples that He must*
> *go to Jerusalem and suffer many things at the hands of the elders,*
> *chief' priests and teachers of the Law, and that He must be killed and*
> *on the third day be raised to life. Peter took Him aside and began to*
> *rebuke Him. "Never, Lord!" he said. "This shall never happen to You!"*
>
> MATTHEW 16:21–22

Jesus responded to Peter's words as an extension of the temptation by Satan (Matthew 4:10) to refuse the path of service, suffering, and death. Maybe, the disciples feared that what would happen to Jesus would also happen to them. In a way, they were right.

> *Then Jesus said to His disciples, "If anyone would come after Me, he*
> *must deny himself and take up his cross and follow Me. For whoever*
> *wants to save his life will lose it, but whoever loses his life for Me will*
> *find it. What good will it be for a man if he gains the whole world, yet*
> *forfeits his soul? Or what can a man give in exchange for his soul?*
>
> MATTHEW 16:24–26

Was Jesus thinking of Augustus whose temple he faced? Here was a man who had conquered and controlled the largest empire since Alexander the Great. Surely, if anyone had ever "gained the whole world," it was Augustus. Yet, there was One greater than Augustus here. Unlike the Roman emperors who were proclaimed as "gods," the God of Israel showed Himself to humanity as the lowly Jesus of Nazareth. In the end, He will rule over all authorities and prove to be the greatest power of all. Speaking of Jesus, Peter wrote,

...who has gone into Heaven and is at the right hand of God, with
angels, authorities, and powers having been subjected to Him.

1 PETER 3:22

Caesarea Philippi beacons us to trust that Jesus is God. He took His disciples on a two-day walking journey to ask them one question—who do you say I am? With the bustling pagan city in the background, reminding us of New York or Las Vegas today, His question calls them to trust Him over every other thing. So also, we too must lay aside idols of our heart—false securities or centers of pleasure—and trust that Christ truly has the authority and power to rule over our lives.

TEL DAN

THE SECOND EDEN WITH A FIRM WARNING

The snorting of the enemy's horses is heard from Dan; at the
neighing of their stallions the whole land trembles.

JEREMIAH 8:16

BACKGROUND, ARCHAEOLOGY, AND SIGNIFICANCE

BACKGROUND

Upon seeing Dan for the first time, you may have to remind yourself that you are in Israel. Visitors immediately notice the tangled jungle of trees, the water tumbling down small waterfalls, ancient oaks and pistachio trees towering overhead, and thick carpets of moss and maidenhair ferns. The spies' report back to the tribe of Dan was true: It is a land that wants for nothing (Judges 18:10).

The ancient site of Dan now lies within a nature reserve, protecting the largest tributary of the Jordan River. The source of the water is a spring fed by rain and melting snow from Mount Hermon.

When you ascend to the top of the tel (mound), the ancient site is under your feet. You realize as you look around at the mountains that this is a protected and strategic location for a city. It was the first line of defense on Israel's northern border.

THE HISTORY OF DAN

Dan has been called "Israel's Garden of Eden." As you would expect in such a paradise, people came to live by the springs of Dan around 5000 B.C. The first true city was built here in about 2800 B.C. and continued to prosper for the next eight centuries. Although the population decreased around 2000 B.C., the city continued to be inhabited. About 1750 B.C., the inhabitants built massive defensive ramparts and the mudbrick city gate for protection.

The original name of the city was "Laish", the name by which it is known in Egyptian records. Its mention in Egyptian texts is a sign of economic and political power for the Canaanite city

QUICK FACTS

Tel Dan was first inhabited around 5,000 B.C.

The waters here form the headwaters of the Jordan River.

Originally called Laish, it was a great Canaanite city before Israel's arrival.

Dan continued to be used as a religious center well into the Roman period.

REFERENCES

Genesis 14:14; 49:16–17

Deuteronomy 33:22; 34:1

Joshua 19:47

Judges 18; 20:1

1 Samuel 3:20

2 Samuel 3:10; 17:11; 24:2, 15

1 Kings 4:25; 12:26–30; 15:20

2 Kings 10:29

1 Chronicles 12:35; 21:2; 27:22

2 Chronicles 2:14; 16:4; 30:5

Jeremiah 4:15; 8:16

Ezekiel 48:1–2, 32

Amos 8:14

in the 1700s B.C. The Egyptian pharaoh, Thutmose III, conquered the city in 1468 B.C.

DAN IN THE BIBLE

Laish continued in prosperity and security until the tribe of Dan captured and renamed it. Although they were originally allotted territory in the Shephelah, they moved north to this site. Jonathan, a Levite, became the priest for the city, setting up an image stolen from another religious shrine in Ephraim (Judges 18).

At least by the time of Saul, Dan was considered the northernmost city occupied by the Israelites, hence the biblical saying, "from Dan to Beersheba," meaning from north to south. The city was also known as a cult center. In the early days of the Divided Kingdom, Jeroboam I of the northern kingdom set up a golden calf here as well as in Bethel.

Dan was destroyed by the Arameans under their king Ben-Hadad I. King Ahab of Israel later rebuilt the city after defeating Ben-Hadad. When the Assyrian army, under Tiglath-Pileser III, invaded Israel, Dan was the first site to be captured. The last mention of the site in the Bible was from Jeremiah who warned that further destruction was coming.

THE ARCHAEOLOGY OF DAN

The abundant springs and fertile ground attracted people to the area for several thousand years. By 2800 B.C., the city was already large by the standards of that time (about 50 acres) and quite prosperous. The tel of Dan is now 65 feet above the level of the plain (the result of repeated rebuilding of the city in the same location).

The next massive building period was in the Middle Bronze period around 1750 B.C. The site was fortified with massive ramparts of dirt piled up against a core of stones or mud brick. It has been estimated that 800,000 tons of material was moved to build these ramparts. The slope of 40 degrees was meant to deny an attacker an easy approach to the city wall, which would have been built on top of the ramparts.

Two towers on either side of the triple-arched entrance protected the gate. This was built 1,500 years before the first Roman arch. Imported ceramics, ivory, gold and silver jewelry, and a well-built palace show that the city was prosperous. Danite spies described the city as "...lacking nothing whatever" (Judges 18:10). No doubt, an abrupt change in the archaeological remains corresponds to the arrival of the Danites about 1200 B.C.

The new residents lived in temporary dwellings such as tents or huts, using jars made just like those in their original territory in the Judean hill country. They eventually erected houses of stones and became involved in metalworking. No remains have been found of the original sanctuary where Jonathan set up the images stolen from the house of Micah (Judges 18:14–31). This incident, however, undoubtedly set a precedent for later cult activity at Dan.

About 925 B.C., the Israelite king Jeroboam I built a sanctuary at Dan and placed a golden calf there to divert religious and political loyalty away from Jerusalem (1 Kings 12:30). Remains of this sanctuary have been uncovered, but only the large rectangular platform remains (modern steel beams are erected there to give you a visualization of what size this sanctuary would have been). The nearby storerooms confirmed that this was a cultic area since they contained a decorated incense stand, chalices for offerings, and figurines.

King Ahab was probably responsible for constructing the thick city wall and strong gateway since he feared an attack from the Arameans. It was also during the time of Ahab that the cult area was enlarged to twice its original size. A four-horned altar and incense shovels were found near this sacred area.

Dan continued to exist even after the Assyrians conquered the city. The building of ordinary homes continued until the Babylonian conquest, and the site continued to be used as a religious shrine well into the Roman period.

WHAT CAN WE LEARN FROM DAN?

GOD WARNS AND CORRECTS THOSE HE LOVES

A voice is announcing from Dan, proclaiming disaster from the hills
of Ephraim. "Tell this to the nations, proclaim it to Jerusalem: A
besieging army is coming from a distant land, raising a war against the
cities of Judah. They surround her like men guarding a field, because
she has rebelled against Me," declares the LORD.

JEREMIAH 4:15–17

The judgment and punishment of God are unpleasant subjects, and it is easy to shy away from them. However, these are prominent themes in the prophets; one of their symbols of judgment is the city of Dan. The name Dan means "judge."

Dan has much to teach us about the nature of God's judgment. The city of Dan struggled at several points with idolatry. While God's judgment is sure, it does not necessarily come swiftly or according to a specified timetable.

Jeremiah warned that the land of Judah was about to be judged, and the announcement of its coming would first be heard in Dan.

> *The snorting of the enemy's horses is heard from Dan; at the neighing*
> *of their stallions the whole land trembles. They have come to devour*
> *the land and everything in it, the city and all who live there.*
>
> JEREMIAH 8:16

The stories of warning and judgment also serve a positive purpose. The apostle Paul discussed the topic of judgment by pointing to examples from Israel's history:

> *Now these things occurred as examples to keep us from setting our*
> *hearts on evil things as they did... These things happened to them as*
> *examples and were written down as warnings for us, on whom the*
> *fulfillment of the ages has come.*
>
> 1 CORINTHIANS 10:6, 11

We can come to understand that the warnings of God are an act of grace. Like parents, who warn their children about harmful activities, God uses examples to keep us away from wrongdoing. While we may not like to think of our God as firm, a disciplinarian, or imposing judgment, this is part of His nature. He will take care of His children by keeping their best interests in mind. At the same time, He is zealous for His own glory and will protect it at any cost.

The Bible is clear that "Blessed is the man You discipline, O LORD, the man You teach from Your law" (Psalm 94:12; Deuteronomy 8:5; 1 Corinthians 11:32). There will be times in our lives when God warns, directs, or disciplines us to prevent our wandering from His plan for our lives. Like the people of Dan, our destruction is inevitable if we choose to walk in prideful disobedience apart from God. However, God is quick to give grace and peace to the humble and obedient (1 Peter 5:5).

THE JORDAN RIVER

THE GREAT DIVIDE

Then Jesus came from Galilee to the Jordan to be baptized by John.

MATTHEW 3:13

BACKGROUND, ARCHAEOLOGY, AND SIGNIFICANCE

BACKGROUND

The Jordan River has its source at the base of Mount Hermon, tumbling from the rocks and springs in a paradise-like setting. As it exits the Sea of Galilee to the south, the river is about 50 feet across, lined with lush eucalyptus trees. The river would have been much wider in biblical times. Today, the National Water Carrier diverts 72,000 cubic meters of water every hour from the Sea of Galilee to the drier southern areas of the country.

THE DESCRIPTION OF THE RIVER

The name Jordan, or yarden in Hebrew, means "river that descends." From the time it leaves its main sources at the foot of Mount Hermon, it drops 2,600 feet to the Dead Sea, the lowest point on the earth's surface.

The main sources of the river are from the runoff from Mount Hermon and the springs near Dan and Caesarea Philippi. As the river runs toward the Sea of Galilee, the volume of water increases as several small tributaries and springs contribute to the flow. After leaving the Sea of Galilee, it meanders 200 miles (75 miles in a straight line) to the Dead Sea.

The scorching temperatures and lack of rainfall south of the Sea of Galilee make much of the flood plain a desolate wasteland. The course of the river runs well below the level of the flood plain, making it difficult to use the water for irrigation. However, the banks of the river are lined with vegetation. This tangled mass of bushes, tamarisks, and semi-tropical trees is referred to in Jeremiah.

The Jordan River has its headwaters at the foot of Mount Hermon.

It drops 2,600 feet in elevation to the Dead Sea, the lowest dry point on earth.

For most of history, crossing had to be done at one of 55 shallow fords.

In the spring, even these fords became impassable.

REFERENCES

Genesis 13:10–11; 32:10; 50:10–11

Numbers 13:29; 22:1; 26:3; 31:12; 32–35; 36:13

Deuteronomy 1:15; 2:29; 3; 4; 6:1; 9:1; 11; 12:10; 27; 30:18; 31; 32:47

Joshua 1–4; 5:1; 7:7; 9; 12–24

Judges 3:28; 5:17; 6:33; 7:24–25; 8:4; 10–12

1 Samuel 13:7; 31:7

2 Samuel 2:29; 10:17; 17:21–24; 19; 20:2; 24:5

1 Kings 2:8; 7:46; 17:3–5

2 Kings 2; 5; 6; 7:15; 10:33

1 Chronicles 6:78; 12; 19:17; 26:30

2 Chronicles 4:17

Job 40:23

Psalm 42:6; 114:3–5

Isaiah 9:1

Jeremiah 12:5; 49:19; 50:44

Zechariah 11:3

Ezekiel 47:18

Matthew 3; 4; 19:1

Luke 3:3; 4:1

Mark 1; 3:8; 10:1

John 1:28; 3:26; 10:40

If you have raced with men on foot and they have worn you out, how can you compete with horses? If you stumble in safe country, how will you manage in the thickets by the Jordan?

JEREMIAH 12:5

Lions and other wild beasts used to be plentiful in the jungle along the Jordan (2 Kings 17:24–28). Wolves, hyenas, foxes, and wild boars call that jungle their home today.

The depth of the river varies by season and by region, from three feet to more than 12 feet. Today, there are two bridges crossing the river; historically, it had to be forded or crossed by boat. Until the nineteenth century, there were 55 shallow fords. In wartime, these fords were guarded to prevent enemies from escaping across the river.

The Jordan comes to an end at the Dead Sea. The river that begins with the breathtaking beauty of Mount Hermon ends with the breathtaking desolation of the lowest point on earth.

THE JORDAN RIVER IN THE OLD TESTAMENT

The Jordan River appears prominently in the Old Testament. Lot, Abraham's nephew, preferred the well-watered plain of the Jordan to the barren Negev hill country.

And Lot lifted up his eyes and saw that the Jordan Valley was well watered everywhere like the garden of the Lord, like the land of Egypt, in the direction of Zoar. (This was before the Lord destroyed Sodom and Gomorrah.)

GENESIS 13:10

When Mesopotamian kings conquered the kings of Sodom and Gomorrah, they took Lot with them. Abram crossed the Jordan River and rescued Lot.

Later, the act of crossing the Jordan was important to Jacob. He first crossed the river with only a staff in his hand, and then returned with a large family and flocks (Genesis 32:10). At the ford near the Jabbok River, Jacob wrestled with God, and his name was changed to Israel.

After the Exodus from Egypt, the twelve spies sent by Moses reported Canaanites living along the Jordan (Numbers 13:29). The failure of the people to trust God at that point resulted in a forty-year delay in seeing the Jordan again.

When Joshua and the Israelites camped on the eastern side of the Jordan, the river presented a formidable obstacle. When the spies who went to Jericho left the city, their pursuers rushed to the Jordan to prevent them from crossing (Joshua 2:7).

The next crossing was a step of faith. When the priests carrying the Ark of the Covenant stepped into the water, the river stopped flowing, allowing the Israelites to cross over.

During the period of the Judges, the river was defended twice in order to capture fugitives. Gideon, along with the tribe of Ephraim, stationed themselves at the waters of the Jordan to cut off the Midianites from escaping (Judges 7:24). In a later period of civil war, the judge Jephthah used the identical maneuver against their brothers the Ephraimites (Judges 12:4–6).

During the reign of King David, his son Absalom led a rebellion, which forced David to flee Jerusalem and cross the Jordan. After Absalom's death, David's crossing of the river symbolized the resumption of his reign (2 Samuel 19:15; 20:2).

The Jordan River played a prominent role in the lives of Elijah and his disciple Elisha. Elijah used his mantle to part the Jordan River (2 Kings 2:8), and the two of them walked across on dry ground. It was by the banks of the Jordan that Elisha requested a double portion of Elijah's spirit just moments before a chariot of fire carried Elijah away. Picking up the mantle, a mourning Elisha returned to the river. He struck the river, and God parted the waters again (2 Kings 2:12–14).

The river plays a slightly less important role in the New Testament, but the stories of Elijah and Elisha parallel those of John the Baptist the New Testament prophet. John the Baptist preached in the wilderness, calling for the people of Israel to repent, and he baptized them in the Jordan. The earthly ministry of Jesus also began here.

> As soon as Jesus was baptized, He went up out of the water. At that moment Heaven was opened, and he saw the Spirit of God descending like a dove and lighting on Him. And a voice from Heaven said, "This is My Son, whom I love; with Him I am well pleased."
>
> MATTHEW 3:16–17

At the Jordan, the people of Israel entered the Promised Land to claim their kingdom. Jesus began His ministry at the same river, announcing the coming of the Kingdom of God.

WHAT CAN WE LEARN FROM THE JORDAN RIVER?

After 40 years of wandering, the situation must have looked grim to the multitude of Israelites standing at the bank of the Jordan. For most of the year, crossing the river required shallow fords. Since the river was in full flood, crossing anywhere was next to impossible. It appeared to be exactly the wrong time.

> So when the people set out from their tents to pass over the Jordan with the priests bearing the ark of the covenant before the people, and as soon as those bearing the ark had come as far as the Jordan, and the feet of the priests bearing the ark were dipped in the brink of the water (now the Jordan overflows all its banks throughout the time of harvest), the waters coming down from above stood and rose up in a heap very far away, at Adam, the city that is beside Zarethan, and those flowing down toward the Sea of the Arabah, the Salt Sea, were completely cut off. And the people passed over opposite Jericho.
>
> JOSHUA 3:14–16 ESV

So often in the Bible, God demonstrates His power and glory by taking charge of seemingly impossible situations. He uses impossible situations to show that His power, not our ingenuity, is at work.

It was true at the Red Sea as the Israelites escaped Egypt. It was true for Sarah, whose miraculous conception of Isaac proved God would always keep His promises. It was true for Gideon when God instructed him to eliminate most of his army so God would receive glory for the victory.

And, it was certainly true when a grave was found empty, and the risen Son of God demonstrated His power over sin and death.

Each day, our challenges take on new forms. God still wants us to trust Him, even when we think that His timing could not be worse. It is then that God may be preparing to show us that everything is under His control.

When God acts on our behalf, we may learn another lesson from Joshua—the lesson of remembrance.

> And Joshua said to them, "Pass on before the ark of the LORD your God into the midst of the Jordan, and take up each of you a stone upon his shoulder, according to the number of the tribes of the people of Israel, that this may be a sign among you. When your children ask in time to come, 'What do those stones mean to you?' then you shall tell them that the waters of the Jordan were cut off before the ark of the covenant of the LORD. When it passed over the Jordan, the waters of the Jordan were cut off. So these stones shall be to the people of Israel a memorial forever."
>
> JOSHUA 4:5–7 ESV

Many of us can remember special occasions when God has done something for us. This may have been a special provision at a crucial time. It might have been deliverance from an impossibly bad situation, or it's possible that it was the moment that you became a Christian. Perhaps, at the time, you promised never to forget.

It might be helpful to do as the Israelites did. Set up a visible reminder in your own life of God's power and mercy. With such a reminder, we can remember and take comfort. Just as God protected or provided for us in the past, He is able to do the same for us again.

TEL HAZOR

HEAD OF THE CANAANITE COALITION

Hazor had been the head of all these kingdoms.

JOSHUA 11:10

BACKGROUND, ARCHAEOLOGY, AND SIGNIFICANCE

BACKGROUND

As the road from the Sea of Galilee curves around to pass by a flat-topped mound (tel), you will get your first glimpse of Hazor. This was the most important city in the region prior to the entry of the Israelites into Galilee. The mound is 130 feet high with over 23 different layers of cities. There are two parts to the tel (the mound formed by city layers). The upper part is 30 acres, while the lower part is comprised of 170 acres and normally grows wheat.

The view from the top of the tel, and its position at the entrance into the Huleh Valley, made Hazor a strategic location. As you look east, your eyes will be attracted to the snow-capped peaks of Mount Hermon. In the wettest seasons, the plains stretching north and south contain hundreds of acres of ponds. These wetlands near Lake Huleh are an important sanctuary for birds along their migratory route between Europe and Africa.

HAZOR IN THE OLD TESTAMENT

Hazor was the largest and one of the most important Canaanite cities. There was a good reason for this; Hazor was located on a branch of the major international road from Egypt and Phoenicia to Assyria. Located eight miles north of the Sea of Galilee, Hazor is mentioned in external sources from several surrounding nations.

By the time the Israelites faced the people of Hazor in battle, the city was the undisputed head of all other Canaanite cities. During Joshua's conquests, Jabin, king of Hazor, headed a league of Canaanite cities (Joshua 11:1–11). Joshua defeated the Canaanite coalition and burned the city.

QUICK FACTS

Hazor was at one time, the largest Canaanite city.

It was located on the major trade route between Egypt and Assyria.

Hazor was destroyed by Joshua and again by Deborah and Barak in Judges.

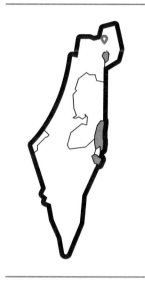

REFERENCES

Matthew 2:22-23; 13:53-58; 21:11

Mark 1:9,24; 6:1-6; 14:67

Luke 1:26-38; 2:4,39,51; 4:15-30

John 1:45-46; 19:19

Acts 10:38

The Canaanites apparently resettled the ruins and regained control of the city. Another Canaanite king, Jabin, ruled Hazor during the period of the Judges. Deborah and Barak defeated Jabin and his general Sisera (Judges 4:1–24).

During the next few centuries, the city was occupied by people living in tents or huts rather than houses. King Solomon fortified Hazor along with other strategic sites (1 Kings 9:15). The city served as a military supply depot and administrative center under the Israelite kings Omri and Ahab. During their reign, several important building projects were undertaken, including a palace with columns, administrative buildings, a storehouse, and water supply system.

The city was once destroyed by fire and was reconstructed when yet another disaster hit, this time an earthquake in 763 B.C. Jeroboam II rebuilt Hazor with extraordinarily thick walls. Even then, it was soon destroyed by the Assyrians.

Israelite occupation of the site ended during the reign of Pekah, King of Israel, when the Assyrian King, Tiglath-Pileser III destroyed it in 732 B.C. (2 Kings 15:29). Its inhabitants were exiled, and never again did Israelites occupy the city. A series of citadels and forts were built and abandoned over the next 400 years, but there are no more mentions of Hazor in the Bible.

THE ARCHAEOLOGY OF HAZOR

Hazor is the largest ancient tel (mound) in the Holy Land. Excavations began in 1938 and still continue today. Descriptions of the finds fill volumes of excavation reports. The earliest settlers, attracted by the perennial spring to the south, arrived in about 2800 B.C. Little remains from that time except pottery. By 2000 B.C., semi-nomadic people were living at Hazor.

When commercial relations between Egypt and Babylon were at their peak, the city conducted a massive building campaign. Hazor expanded about 200 acres to the north and was fortified for the first time. A large earthen rampart served as the foundation of the city wall. The dirt for the rampart was removed from the area in front, forming a large ditch for additional protection. The inhabitants built several temples and two palaces, one in the upper city and one in the lower city. Hazor's prosperity ended with its violent destruction, probably by the Egyptians in about 1500 B.C.

Atop the ashes, a new Canaanite city arose. In this period, a shrine was built and is now on display in the Israel Museum (replicas are located in the Hazor Museum across the street from the tel). In addition to the shrine was a temple, built on a plan similar to that of the Temple in Jerusalem.

When the lower part of the city was destroyed between 1250 and 1200 B.C., it was never inhabited again. The destruction was so complete that through the years, this area was used to cultivate crops. In fact, this lower area was thought by early archaeologists to be a parking lot for Solomon's chariots and a camping ground for his infantry.

WHAT CAN WE LEARN FROM TEL HAZOR?

IF AT FIRST YOU DON'T SUCCEED...

One of the first things we notice about Hazor in the Old Testament is the conquest of the city, first by Joshua and then two centuries later in the book of Judges. Why did Israel have to destroy the city twice? Although God gave His people the mandate to take the land, they were not always successful.

Unfortunately, our victories are not always permanent, and it's easy to find spiritual parallels in our own lives. Sometimes, the 'enemy' we defeated – a particular temptation, thought pattern, or habit – comes back to haunt us long after we thought that the issue was defeated.

When it comes to fighting battles with our sin or the enemy, we have to fight the battle more than once to win it.

Perhaps, Hazor was in too good a location to be given up by the enemy. Perhaps, the Israelites had later 'cut a deal' with some of the Canaanites to resettle the area. Perhaps, the Israelites were not paying attention to the resettlement of what was previously a stronghold of the enemy. In any case, a single victory over a strong enemy turned out to be insufficient.

Scripture contains numerous warnings to Christians to remain strong in their faith and not return to sins in which they had been previously involved. Sin can so easily come back to wage war on us a second time if we are not vigilant.

However, God has not left us without weapons. Paul gave this warning and encouragement to the Corinthians who struggled with idolatry in the past.

So, if you think you are standing firm, be careful that you don't fall!
No temptation has seized you except what is common to man. And God

is faithful; He will not let you be tempted beyond what you can bear.
But when you are tempted, He will also provide a way out so that you
can stand up under it.

1 CORINTHIANS 10:12–13

When it comes to fighting temptation or even getting through trials in life, we may have to fight the battle more than once to win it. However, we know that there is a Savior in Jesus who identifies with our weaknesses (Heb. 4:15-16). We can approach His throne with confidence that He will give us the grace and mercy we need to keep fighting to win, for His glory.

SEA OF GALILEE
THE STAGE OF JESUS' MINISTRY

Even the wind and the waves obey him!

MATTHEW 8:27

BACKGROUND, ARCHAEOLOGY, AND SIGNIFICANCE

BACKGROUND

The Sea of Galilee is a beautiful freshwater lake shaped like a harp. Its Hebrew name, Yam Kinneret, comes from the word "kinnor," which means "harp". It was also known as the Lake of Tiberias after the nearby city built by Herod Antipas. "Galilee," the name by which the lake is known in the Gospels, means "ring" in Hebrew. This comes from the surrounding mountains on all sides except the north.

The plains to the west, northeast, and south are made fertile by deposits from the Jordan River. Numerous springs around the lake add to the fertility of the area. At Tiberias, the hot springs were developed into a spa during the Roman period.

GEOGRAPHY

The Sea of Galilee is fed by the Jordan River, which brings snowmelt from Mount Hermon. Additional water comes from springs around the lake, many of which are hot springs. The hot water allows tropical fish to thrive, and the high rate of evaporation creates a humid environment suitable for tropical plants and fruit to grow. Winter and spring are mild and pleasant while the summers are hot and humid.

The lake is now 12.5 miles long and seven miles wide, but may have been larger in Jesus' time since receding in the north near Bethsaida. The surface of the lake is about 700 feet below sea level.

The town of Bethsaida is located on a plain to the northeast where the Jordan River empties into the lake. This fishing village was the home of Peter and Andrew. James and John may have been from Bethsaida originally, but they ran a thriving

QUICK FACTS

At 700 feet below sea level, the Sea of Galilee creates a humid, tropical environment.

The lake is 12.5 miles long and seven miles wide, but may have been bigger in Jesus' day.

Its location makes it susceptible to violent storms like we saw in the New Testament.

The small coves create natural amphitheaters where Jesus taught.

The Sea of Galilee is where Jesus did many miracles, including calming the storm and walking on water.

REFERENCES

Numbers 34:11

Joshua 12:3; 13:27

Matthew 4:12–22; 8:18 – 9:1; 13:1–35, 47–50

Matthew 14:13, 22–36; 15:29, 39; 16:1–12; 17:24–27; 18:6

Mark 1:16–20; 2:13–14; 3:7–9; 4:1–9; 4:35–5:21

Mark 6:45–56; 7:31; 8:13–21; 9:42

Luke 5:1–11; 8:22–40

John 6:1–25; 21

fishing business from Capernaum. As the Jordan empties organic material into the lake, it creates an excellent environment for fish. It's no coincidence that these well-known fishermen came from this area.

THE SEA OF GALILEE IN THE NEW TESTAMENT

In Jesus' day, the lake was divided between Jewish and Gentile populations. Jewish areas were concentrated from the west around to the northeast. Gentile populations surrounded the rest of the lake. It is important to read the events of the Gospels in light of where they took place around the Sea of Galilee. Some locations are important in understanding the context and method of Jesus' ministry.

> *They went across the lake to the region of*
> *the Gerasenes. When Jesus got out of the*
> *boat, a man with an evil spirit came from*
> *the tombs to meet Him.*
>
> MARK 5:1–2

Jesus cast the demons out of the man and transferred them to a herd of pigs on the hillside. This happened in a Gentile area of the lake, so it's reasonable that a herd of pigs would be kept nearby. Such a miracle never would have happened on the northwestern shore.

When Jesus healed people in Jewish areas on the west side of the Sea of Galilee, he often warned them not to tell anyone.

> *As Jesus went on from there, two blind men*
> *followed Him, calling out, "Have mercy on*
> *us, Son of David."*
>
> *When He had gone indoors, the blind men*
> *came to Him, and He asked them, "Do you*
> *believe that I am able to do this?" "Yes,*

Lord," they replied. Then He touched their eyes and said, "According to
your faith it will be done to you." And their sight was restored. Jesus
warned them sternly, "See that no one knows about this." But they
went out and spread the news about Him all over that region.

MATTHEW 9:27–31

Based on a misunderstanding of why the Messiah would come, Jesus knew there would be a tendency for people in this area to revolt. After His crucifixion and resurrection, it would become clear that the Messiah had come not to overthrow the Roman government, but to die for their sins.

The small coves and bays around the lake provided natural amphitheaters. These would have provided the perfect places for many people to be taught all at once and still be able to hear Jesus, whether he was teaching on land or from the lake.

That same day Jesus went out of the house and sat by the lake. Such
large crowds gathered around Him that He got into a boat and sat in
it, while all the people stood on the shore. Then He told them many
things in parables.

MATTHEW 13:1–3

While the crowds sat on the gentle slopes around the water's edge, Jesus taught from a boat. This took advantage of winds carrying His voice toward shore. At Capernaum, see if you can identify the nearby cove where Jesus would have taught the crowds.

WHAT CAN WE LEARN FROM THE SEA OF GALILEE?

JESUS CALMS THE STORMS ON THE SEA OF GALILEE AND OUR LIFE

A furious squall came up, and the waves broke over the boat, so that
it was nearly swamped. Jesus was in the stern, sleeping on a cushion.
The disciples woke Him and said to Him, "Teacher, don't you care if
we drown?"

He got up, rebuked the wind and said to the waves, "Quiet! Be still!"
Then the wind died down and it was completely calm. He said to His
disciples, "Why are you so afraid? Do you still have no faith?" They

were terrified and asked each other, "Who is this? Even the wind and
the waves obey Him!"

MARK 4:37–41

From December until March, winds can be unpredictable and quickly change. Surrounding air dropping toward the lake can cause storms to be very violent. The Valley of Arbel acts like a wind tunnel, forcing the wind onto the lake. On the eastern side, steep mountain slopes form a barrier, and the wind swirls back over the sea, resulting in huge waves and cloudbursts.

It is important to understand the disciples' perspective in order to make sense of their fear in Mark 4. It was common to view the seas as possessing a power against which people were helpless. The deep ocean was sometimes used as a metaphor for personal danger.

Save me, o God, for the waters have come up to my neck. I sink in
the miry depths, where there is no foothold. I have come into the deep
waters; the floods engulf me.

PSALM 69:1–2

Israel also understood that the sea with its roaring waves were in
God's control. Just as God brought creation out of watery chaos, God
could still the roaring sea.

You answer us with awesome deeds of righteousness, O God our
Savior, the hope of all the ends of the earth and of the farthest seas,
who formed the mountains by Your power, having armed Yourself with
strength, who stilled the roaring of the seas, the roaring of their waves,
and the turmoil of the nations.

PSALM 65:5–7

Even though they were experienced on the sea, the disciples feared for their lives. Jesus' ability to calm the wind and the waves could only mean one thing: God was with them in the boat. Only God Himself could control the sea. They did not yet fully understand who Jesus was when they asked, "Who is this?"

Life often brings challenges and problems that are beyond our control. Our initial reaction may be to panic, bailing out our boat as fast as we can. However, our first reaction should be to turn toward the One who calms the wind and the waves. He has power over creation, power over sin and death, and power over any problem the world can throw at us.

As you look upon the Sea of Galilee, reflect on God's power over the forces that threaten to overwhelm you.

The seas have lifted up, O LORD, the seas have lifted up their voice;
the seas have lifted up their pounding waves. Mightier than the
thunder of the great waters, mightier than the breakers of the sea—the
LORD on high is mighty.

PSALM 93:3–4

CHORAZIN

THE CURSE CITY

Woe to you, Chorazin! Woe to you, Bethsaida! If the miracles that were performed in you had been performed in Tyre and Sidon, they would have repented long ago in sackcloth and ashes.

MATTHEW 11:21

BACKGROUND, ARCHAEOLOGY, AND SIGNIFICANCE

BACKGROUND

Piles of black basalt rocks lie on the ancient site of Chorazin, strewn down a hillside about two miles north of the Sea of Galilee. Bleak and forlorn, Chorazin stands as mute testimony to Jesus' curse uttered almost two thousand years ago. The town began on the hill north of the road near a spring whose location is indicated by the presence of large green bushes. The remains of the city extend on both sides of the modern road, spreading down the hill toward the Sea of Galilee.

Most of the buildings you see were reconstructed along the lines of the fourth century A.D. town. The excavated and reconstructed parts of the city include houses of black basalt, a synagogue, and a public courtyard area. As you look toward the Sea of Galilee, you notice a path lined with fallen stones from houses not yet excavated. This path, should you decide to follow it, leads to Capernaum, which is two and a half miles away.

THE HISTORY OF CHORAZIN

Coins found in the area around Chorazin indicate the town Jesus visited began during the time of the Maccabees, over a century before the time of Christ (though there is evidence people lived near the spring 3,000 years earlier). Like Capernaum, where Jesus spent most of His ministry, Chorazin seems to have been settled by Jews who moved north from Judaea after the military campaigns that brought Galilee back under Jewish control. This village apparently prospered, along with Capernaum, with an increase in trade along the road north of the town. It was during this period of prosperity that Jesus visited Chorazin, preaching and performing miracles.

QUICK FACTS

Chorazin was one of the major Galilean towns at the time of Jesus.

Volcanic rock, called "basalt," is the black stone that makes up much of Chorazin.

Chorazin has one of the clearest remains of a synagogue that we can see today.

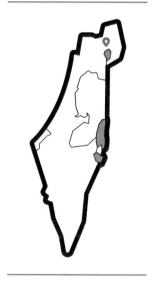

REFERENCES

Matthew 11:20–24

Luke 10:13–16

About a century after Jesus cursed the town for its unbelief (Matthew 11:21), Chorazin was destroyed by the Roman army in reprisal for its participation in the revolt led by Simon Bar Kochba (A.D. 132–135). The town was later rebuilt on the ruins of the former village and expanded toward the south. The new town boasted a synagogue, a plaza area, and houses built along the intersecting streets.

Chorazin did not enjoy prosperity for long, for it was again destroyed toward the end of the fourth century A.D. Its destruction was, perhaps, a result of the religious animosity that prevailed in the area during the middle of the fourth century. Although Constantine the Great legalized Christianity in A.D. 313, his rule, and that of his sons, was followed by Julian, who opposed Christians. Julian supported Jewish causes and even attempted to rebuild the temple in Jerusalem in an attempt to weaken Christianity. After Julian's death in A.D. 363, there was a wave of Christian attacks against synagogues and the Jewish community in Galilee. The destruction of the synagogue in Chorazin, and part of the town itself, may have been the result of those attacks.

The town was rebuilt again in the fifth century along the lines you see today. Some of the houses have been reconstructed to show how they would have looked before they were, once again, destroyed; in A.D. 747 a catastrophic earthquake destroyed all the towns along the Jordan Rift Valley.

THE ARCHAEOLOGY OF CHORAZIN

The memory of Chorazin remained long after its destruction. It was not until 1869, however, that one area of the ruins was identified as a synagogue. The excavation and restoration of the synagogue, and the rest of the town, has continued periodically from 1905 to today. The synagogue, built of the local black basalt stone, was two stories high, ensuring that its roof was above all others in the town as required by tradition. Its three entrances faced south, the direction of Jerusalem, and it was in this direction that prayers were recited several times daily. Two rows of benches for members of the synagogue were placed around the west, north, and east walls. One of the most important finds from this site was an inscribed stone seat now in the Israel Museum in Jerusalem.

The area west of the synagogue was a residential area of small homes, some of which are reconstructed. As you enter the houses, you are aware how small the interior space was. The arches that were required to support the roof took up much of the room inside, while the presence of only one or two windows for each house reminds visitors it was quite dark inside. Most household chores were performed in the courtyard outside the home.

The houses in the western district of the city are quite different from the insulae or residential complexes on the eastern side of town. The residential complex was of Roman derivation, providing living quarters for an extended family or several families around a communal open area. What appears to be small windows in the middle of rooms are, in fact, supports for the roof.

CHORAZIN IN THE NEW TESTAMENT

Galilee, more than any other region, was the stage for Jesus' teaching and healing ministry. It was in Galilee that the disciples, sent by John the Baptist, found Jesus. They came with a question: Are You the one who was to come, or should we expect someone else? (Matthew 11:2b). In reply, Jesus told them to return to John and report what they had heard and seen.

> *The blind receive sight, the lame walk, those who have leprosy are cleansed, the deaf hear, the dead are raised, and the Good News is preached to the poor.*
>
> MATTHEW 11:5

Where did those cured people live? Primarily in the cities of Chorazin, Bethsaida, and Capernaum. However, even though most of Jesus' miracles were performed in these three cities, they did not turn to God. Jesus preached and healed in these cities more than the others in the area, and so, He held them more accountable for their rejection and cursed them.

> *Woe to you, Chorazin! Woe to you, Bethsaida! For if the mighty works done in you had been done in Tyre and Sidon, they would have repented long ago in sackcloth and ashes. But I tell you, it will be more bearable on the day of judgment for Tyre and Sidon than for you.*
>
> MATTHEW 11:21–22

While excavating at Chorazin, one of the authors gained some insight into the present-day results of that curse. By day, the black volcanic stones radiate the sun's heat, making the ruins even more forlorn and inhospitable. The only sign of life and industry came from the nests of hornets, who were busily warding off the encroachment of archaeologists into their territory.

By night, the surface of the black soil came to life. Large scorpions crawled out from beneath the stones and speedily made their way around the site to find their prey. While the sting of this particular kind of scorpion is not fatal to an adult, the word we received was that their sting would make you wish you were dead. An Israeli volunteer, who was helping on the excavation and after enduring several hornet stings and close encounters with scorpions, said to the author, "I think that there might be something to this curse after all."

SO WHAT CAN WE LEARN FROM CHORAZIN?

And He told them many things in parables, saying: "A sower went out to sow. And as he sowed, some seeds fell along the path, and the birds came and devoured them. Other seeds fell on rocky ground, where they did not have much soil, and immediately they sprang up, since they had no depth of soil, but when the sun rose they were scorched. And since they had no root, they withered away. Other seeds fell among thorns, and the thorns grew up and choked them. Other seeds fell on good soil and produced grain, some a hundredfold, some sixty, some thirty. He who has ears, let him hear."

MATTHEW 13:3–9

When reading the parables of Jesus, it is important to note how they fit the geographical context in which they were told. For example, parables about vines and fig trees were normally spoken of in Judea where these crops are a plentiful and familiar part of the landscape. Parables about wheat farming, on the other hand, belong to the northern part of the country in the fertile valleys and plains around the Sea of Galilee. It was in Galilee that Jesus related the parable of the sower. How does our knowledge of the local geography inform our interpretation of the parable?

As you look at the area around Chorazin, you can see for yourself the types of soil to which Jesus referred. The countryside is strewn with basalt boulders, sometimes with little soil in which seed can grow. A seed thrown into this area will spring up quickly; the black rock around and underneath the soil retains the heat and encourages rapid growth. However, the heat of the sun will prove too much for the seedling, which cannot sink its roots down deeply. Weeds and thistles seem to survive the best, although at the expense of other plants.

The portion of the parable that is rarely discussed is the last part, in which the yield of the crop varies—a hundred, sixty, or thirty times. What causes the difference in the yield? The reason lies neither with the seed itself nor with the sower. Rather, it is due to differences in the soil. While it may not be readily apparent, the dark soil around Chorazin and Capernaum can be very fertile. The soil comes from the slow wearing down of the basalt boulders. The heavy soil washed down from the area above Chorazin also contains a large amount of organic matter from the decomposition of weeds and thistles.

The difficulty in working with this type of soil is that it tends to form hard clods in summer and muddy swamps in the winter. It must be broken up frequently to maintain its fertility. The soil must also receive enough water, but the water cannot be allowed to stay and stagnate; the area must be properly drained.

Like the soil around Chorazin, we must also be broken on occasion
if we are to become fertile fields for God. Years after Jesus told the
parable, the apostle Paul realized that being broken benefitted not only
himself, but others as well—perhaps a hundred, sixty, or thirty times.

For as we share abundantly in Christ's sufferings, so through Christ
we share abundantly in comfort too. If we are afflicted, it is for your
comfort and salvation; and if we are comforted, it is for your comfort,
which you experience when you patiently endure the same sufferings
that we suffer.

2 CORINTHIANS 1:5–6

BETHSAIDA

HOME OF THE DISCIPLES

On their return the apostles told him all that they had done. And he took them and withdrew apart to a town called Bethsaida. When the crowds learned it, they followed him, and he welcomed them and spoke to them of the kingdom of God and cured those who had need of healing.

BACKGROUND, ARCHAEOLOGY, AND SIGNIFICANCE

BETHSAIDA IN HISTORY

According to Josephus, Bethsaida rose in prominence during the first century A.D. At some point in that interval, Bethsaida was recognized as a "polis" and was renamed "Bethsaida Julias" in honor of the Emperor Augustus' daughter.

Bethsaida's location on top of a black basalt volcanic rock made it especially conducive for building defenses. Some sources believe Bethsaida was originally called "Zer," meaning "rocks" after its rocky perch. Scholars speculate that this very fact inspired Jesus to draw a connection between Peter's confession of faith and the "rock" of his hometown (Matt. 16:18).

THE ARCHAEOLOGY OF BETHSAIDA

The ancient city Bethsaida is believed to be under the modern city et-Tell, although some archaeologists and historians dispute this location. Beginning in 1987, excavations near the site of the ancient city yielded a plethora of articles from the second Iron Age and early Roman. Uncovered finds such as anchors, hooks, and net weights make up the find. The discovery of "non-kosher faunal remains," including pig, suggests a Gentile contingency also resided in Bethsaida along with its Jewish inhabitants.

The absence of a synagogue and cisterns used for ritual washing makes the site of ancient Bethsaida unique among those of other ancient Jewish villages. Although it is unwise to draw conclusions about the piety of Bethsaida's residents based on these findings, it is interesting to note Bethsaida's location and proximity in relation to Gentile-centric populations.

QUICK FACTS

Bethsaida is a fishing village situated just over 1.5 miles northeast of the River Jordan's mouth along the Sea of Galilee.

Bethsaida is surrounded by plains full of game and waters full of fish, hence the name "Bethsaida," meaning "house of the hunter/fisherman."

Bethsaida was also home to the apostles Peter, Andrew, and Philip.

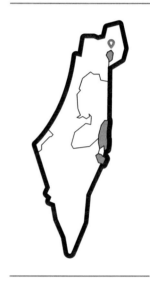

REFERENCES

Matthew 11:21-22

Mark 8:22

Luke 9:10-11

John 1:44, 12:21

It's believed Jesus miraculously fed the crowd of 5,000 and walked on water near Bethsaida (Mark 6:30-44; 45-52). Jesus' healing of the blind man also took place in Bethsaida (Mark 8:22-26). However, Bethsaida is also notable because Jesus specifically condemned this city, along with Chorazin, cursing it for its lack of faith (Matthew 11:21-22).

WHAT CAN WE LEARN FROM BETHSAIDA?

By all accounts, ancient Bethsaida was a modest village, a community of fisherman and hunters, Jews and Gentiles alike. Hailing from Bethsaida would not have afforded fisherman like Peter, Andrew, and Phillip any clout or great opportunities, and, in fact, they were considered "uneducated, common men" (said specifically of Peter and John, Acts 4:13). And yet, these simple fishermen followed Jesus' call to follow Him, which made all the difference for their life and ministry.

The calling of Peter, Andrew, and John, these uneducated Bethsaida boys, reminds us, in the words of Paul, that God often uses:

"But God chose what is foolish in the world to shame the wise; God chose what is weak in the world to shame the strong; God chose what is low and despised in the world, even things that are not, to bring to nothing things that are, so that no human being might boast in the presence of God."

1 CORINTHIANS 1:27-29

We can therefore rejoice that no matter our background, our education, our pedigree, or any man-made pedigree, God chooses and equips us through the Holy Spirit to do good works prepared beforehand (Eph. 2:10). He is faithful to call common men to His uncommon work.

"Therefore, if anyone is in Christ, he is a new creation. The old has passed away; behold, the new has come."

2 CORINTHINANS 5:17

CAPERNAUM

A TEMPORARY HOME FOR JESUS BY THE SEA

The people living in darkness have seen a great light; on those
living in the land of the shadow of death a light has dawned.

MATTHEW 4:16

BACKGROUND, ARCHAEOLOGY AND SIGNIFICANCE:

BACKGROUND

Capernaum was the center of Jesus' ministry and is no longer inhabited. It was abandoned after the Islamic conquest of the seventh century, and then completely ruined after the earthquake of 747 A.D.

It was once a thriving town on the northern shore of the Sea of Galilee. The vibrant colors of the bougainvillea, eucalyptus, and palm trees at the entrance are reminders of the fertility of the soil and the mild climate. Part of the city lies within the walls of the Franciscan compound. The Greek Orthodox Church owns another part of the former city east of the compound.

Much of Capernaum lies unexcavated, eastward along the shore and northward toward the hills. Black basalt stones are visible in the fields, indicating the remains of buildings below the soil. This once-lovely village was home to a white limestone synagogue and basalt houses, evidence of its prosperity over several centuries.

THE ARCHAEOLOGY OF CAPERNAUM

Excavations in Capernaum began with the synagogue in 1866 and continue intermittently to this day. Archaeological remains as old as the third millennium B.C. have been found here. However, the town was abandoned from about 1200 B.C. until the fifth century B.C. Capernaum remained a prosperous Jewish village until the fifth century A.D.

THE SYNAGOGUE

The synagogue was the dominant feature of Capernaum. It was believed that houses built above the synagogue would end in destruction,

QUICK FACTS

Once a thriving town, Capernaum was abandoned in the seventh century A.D.

In many ways, Capernaum served as the home base for Jesus' earthly ministry.

Remnants exist of the synagogue where Jesus taught.

Peter lived in his mother-in-law's home in Capernaum.

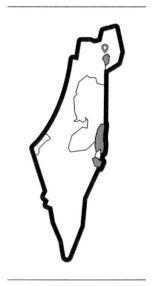

REFERENCES

Matthew 4:12–17; 8:5–22; 9:1–34; 11:20–24; 17:24–27

Mark 1:21–39; 2:1–12; 3:20; 4:34; 9:33–50

Luke 4:23, 31–44; 5:12–39; 7:1–10; 10:13–15

John 2:12; 4:46–54; 6:16–71

so Capernaum's synagogue was built on the highest point in town. The white limestone building that you see today is the fourth-century A.D. structure, built above the remains of the first-century synagogue in which Jesus taught and healed.

The synagogue today is composed of four units: the main prayer hall, a courtyard to the east, a porch on the south, and a room at the back. Benches for the congregation line the two sides of the hall.

The colonnaded courtyard on the east side was the Beit Midrash or "place of teaching". Children were taught here in the morning, and adults came to study after their workday. This is the area where Jesus would have taught.

The only remnants of the synagogue from Jesus' day are the lower walls and basalt pavement. Visitors can best view these remains on the porch near the exit from the courtyard. The later limestone synagogue reused stones from the older synagogue in its foundation.

Additionally, the later synagogue was richly decorated with Greek motifs such as victory wreaths, garlands, and geometric designs, animals, cupids, and birds. Most of these have since been effaced. Jewish motifs included: the menorah, the incense shovel, the shofar (ram's horn), and the palm tree symbolic of Judaea. The stars of David (six-pointed) and Solomon (five-pointed) were also prominent. Parts of buildings containing these symbols are scattered throughout the grounds.

THE HOUSE OF PETER

The house of Peter is near the synagogue. More precisely, it was his mother-in-law's house where Peter came to live. The remains are now on display below the church.

The three concentric octagonal walls belong to the church that was built over Peter's house in the middle of the fifth century A.D. The basalt walls and floors at the lowest level belonged to the original humble dwelling.

Like other houses of the first century, it contained a number of small rooms clustered around courtyards. This type of house, called an "insula," often housed an extended family or more than one family.

Early church tradition held that this was the house of Peter, and several historical facts support this tradition. Aside from fishing hooks found in the home, one room was continually re-plastered, unlike any other in the house. The plastered room became the focus of what can best be described as a house church. Graffiti in several languages (now kept in a museum) referred to Jesus as Lord, Christ, and the Most High God. Some graffiti also refers to Peter.

The continuity of special use from the first century to the fourth century appears to confirm the tradition that this was not only the house of Peter, but also where Jesus stayed during His ministry.

CAPERNAUM IN THE NEW TESTAMENT

Little is known about Capernaum other than its prominent place in Jesus' ministry. It is often thought that He began His ministry in Nazareth, the first place that He is recorded to have announced Himself publicly as the Messiah.

> *And the scroll of the prophet Isaiah was given to Him. He unrolled the scroll and found the place where it was written, "The Spirit of the Lord is upon Me, because He has anointed Me to proclaim Good News to the poor. He has sent Me to proclaim liberty to the captives and recovering of sight to the blind, to set at liberty those who are oppressed, to proclaim the year of the Lord's favor." And He rolled up the scroll and gave it back to the attendant and sat down. And the eyes of all in the synagogue were fixed on Him. And He began to say to them, "Today this Scripture has been fulfilled in your hearing."*
>
> LUKE 4:17–21

However, the same passage indicates that His Messianic work had already begun in Capernaum.

> *Jesus said to them, "Surely you will quote this proverb to Me: 'Physician, heal yourself! Do here in your hometown what we have heard that you did in Capernaum.'"*
>
> LUKE 4:23

Beyond this statement, we do not know anything about Jesus' earliest ministry in Capernaum.

Matthew 4:13 also tells us that after He was tempted in the wilderness, Jesus went back to Galilee and went to live in Capernaum. From this time forward, Jesus called Capernaum his home.

In Jesus' ministry, Capernaum seems to have been a place for healing. As mentioned earlier, His healing ministry began at Capernaum even before His rejection at Nazareth. Many more healing miracles were ascribed to

Capernaum. These include the healing of Peter's mother-in-law, the healing of a paralytic, a man possessed by demons, a leper, and the raising of Jairus' daughter from the dead.

Three of the Gospel writers also mention the healing of the centurion's servant. It was this centurion that donated the synagogue of Jesus' day, the foundations of which you can see today.

WHAT CAN WE LEARN FROM CAPERNAUM?

THE PURPOSE OF JESUS' MIRACLES

Capernaum played a prominent role in the life of Jesus. It was a virtually unknown fishing town on the north shore of the Sea of Galilee that served as the stage for a large part of Jesus' life. No one would have guessed this discrete town would provide the primary backdrop for the Messiah's ministry. Yet, through God's divine choice, Capernaum was one of three towns Jesus singled out for judgment. He cursed it, comparing the town to Sodom.

> *And you, Capernaum, will you be exalted to Heaven? You will be*
> *brought down to Hades. For if the mighty works done in you had been*
> *done in Sodom, it would have remained until this day. But I tell you*
> *that it will be more tolerable on the Day of Judgment for the land of*
> *Sodom than for you.*
>
> MATTHEW 11:23–24

Witnessing great works of God is no guarantee for great spiritual improvement. As humans, we are tenaciously resistant to change, even when witnessing a miracle.

When we look at the miracles of Jesus, we tend to assume their purpose was to convince people that He was the Messiah, to authenticate His message, or to draw attention to Himself and His teaching. Those reasons are valid, but in Matthew 11:20, we learn that Jesus was looking for a changed life.

> *Then Jesus began to denounce the cities in which most of His miracles*
> *had been performed, because they did not repent.*
>
> MATTHEW 11:20

Peter closely watched his master. He understood the connection between miraculous signs and the call to discipleship. One such miracle that Peter performed, after Jesus' resurrection, was the healing of a beggar at the gate of the temple. Peter responded to the man's request for money.

> *Then Peter said, "Silver or gold I do not have, but what I have I give*
> *you. In the name of Jesus Christ of Nazareth, walk." Taking him by the*
> *right hand, he helped him up, and instantly the man's feet and ankles*
> *became strong.*
>
> ACTS 3:6–7

Peter used the resulting attention as an opportunity to preach the message as Jesus would have preached it.

> *Repent, then, and turn to God, so that your sins may be wiped out,*
> *that times of refreshing may come from the Lord.*
>
> ACTS 3:19

Like the people of Capernaum, who witnessed miracles and failed to undergo a personal transformation, it is easy for us to overlook the touch of God's hand in own lives. Let's be conscious of His work, and give Him thanks and praise. Most importantly, let us worship Him for His ultimate miracle in the death and resurrection in Jesus Christ.

> *He Himself bore our sins in His body on the tree, that we might die to*
> *sin and live to righteousness. By His wounds you have been healed.*
>
> 1 PETER 2:24–25

MOUNT ARBEL

THE RETURN OF THE KING

As Shalman destroyed Beth Arbel on the day of battle...

HOSEA 10:14

BACKGROUND, ARCHAEOLOGY, AND SIGNIFICANCE

BACKGROUND

Nothing quite prepares you for the dramatic view you will encounter while ascending the field to the northwest of Mount Arbel. As you pause at the edge of the sheer limestone cliff, the Sea of Galilee spreads out below you like a smooth carpet. At the foot of Arbel is the little fishing village of Magdala. On a clear day, the plains of Gennesaret and Bethsaida are easily visible as well as Capernaum, the center of Jesus' ministry. As you look across the ravine toward the west, you will see caves on the cliff face opposite you. These caves have a dramatic history.

THE HISTORY OF ARBEL

The first mention of the site of Arbel is in the book of Hosea. The capture of the town by Shalman must have been very devastating and cruel. Unfortunately, the only mention of "Shalman" is in Hosea 10:14; it may refer to Shalmaneser, for there were several Assyrian kings by this name. Shalmaneser V was the king who began the siege of Samaria in 722 B.C. The name might also refer to a Moabite king who is listed along with Jehoahaz of Judah as paying tribute to the Assyrian king Tiglath-Pileser III.

The ridge across from Mount Arbel is riddled with caves, which have been used in numerous revolts. In 160 B.C., Judas Maccabee and his forces fortified and hid out in the caves until the onslaught by the Seleucid general Bacchides. Josephus says that Bacchides besieged and captured Jews who had fled into the nearby caves (Antiquities 12.11). When Herod the Great conquered Palestine, Jewish zealots again used the caves. The result was the same; the zealots were

Mount Arbel is the highest point around the Sea of Galilee.

It has a 360-foot vertical drop and is the only place in Israel with a base-jumping site.

There are documented Jewish cliff dwellings dating back to the Second Temple period.

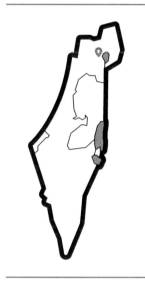

REFERENCES

Hosea 10:14

captured. In A.D. 66, during the First Revolt against Rome, rebels hid out in the caves, but again were eventually captured.

From your eagle's view of Galilee, you can see how the people felt "ringed in" or "encircled," which is the meaning of the word "Galilee." The pressure from invaders into Israel was felt most intensely here. Over the centuries, the wrath of various kingdoms would break in full fury upon the people of Galilee. Aramaeans, several campaigns of Assyrians, Babylonians, Seleucids, Parthians, Romans, Herod—so many conquerors, so much suffering.

To the prophet Hosea, Arbel itself seemed to symbolize the brutality of such invasions, as mothers and children were thrown from the cliffs to their deaths:

> *...the roar of battle will rise against your people, so that all your*
> *fortresses will be devastated—as Shalman devastated Beth Arbel*
> *on the day of battle, when mothers were dashed to the ground with*
> *their children.*

HOSEA 10:14

THE ARCHAEOLOGY OF ARBEL

The remains of the ancient village of Arbela may be seen to the northwest of the moshav, or cooperative farm, through which you drive to get to the entrance of Mount Arbel. The remains of a synagogue and some houses of the Roman period were found there. Nearby are some ruined walls belonging to the fortress Josephus built while he was commander of the Jewish forces in Galilee.

WHAT CAN WE LEARN FROM ARBEL?

THE KINGDOM OF LOVE

Knowing the history of this cliff and of the caves, it seems from this vantage point that kingdoms are established and perpetuated more by violence than by peaceful means. Time after time, contests for lordship in the region were won by the general with the largest army. The caves across the ravine saw the lengths to which Herod went to make the entire region submit to his kingship. Many people who resisted were dragged out with hooks and thrown to their deaths. Lowered in cages from the top of the mountain, soldiers threw torches into the caves and burned countless people to death. Others were thrust through with swords. Time and time again, kingdoms are won by lions, not by lambs.

Everyone's dream of building a kingdom seemed to include the residents of Galilee, and they were the ones who always suffered the most in such efforts. Isaiah, however, described the delivery of the Galileans from this situation.

But there will be no gloom for her who was in anguish. In the former time he brought into contempt the land of Zebulun and the land of Naphtali, but in the latter time he has made glorious the way of the sea, the land beyond the Jordan, Galilee of the nations.

> *The people who walked in darkness have seen a great light; those who dwelt in a land of deep darkness, on them has light shone.*
>
> *You have multiplied the nation; You have increased its joy; they rejoice before You as with joy at the harvest, as they are glad when they divide the spoil.*
>
> *For the yoke of His burden, and the staff for His shoulder, the rod of His oppressor, You have broken as on the day of Midian.*
>
> *For every boot of the tramping warrior in battle tumult and every garment rolled in blood will be burned as fuel for the fire.*
>
> *For to us a Child is born, to us a Son is given; and the government shall be upon his shoulder, and His name shall be called*
>
> *Wonderful Counselor, Mighty God, Everlasting Father, Prince of Peace.*
>
> *Of the increase of His government and of peace there will be no end, on the throne of David and over His kingdom,*
>
> *to establish it and to uphold it with justice and with righteousness from this time forth and forevermore.*
>
> *The zeal of the LORD of hosts will do this.*
>
> ISAIAH 9:1–7

Herod, like so many before him, built a kingdom at Galilee's expense. But, there was another king who brought the message of a kingdom into Galilee: Jesus of Nazareth.

Jesus' way of building a kingdom contrasted dramatically with Herod's. Imagine yourself as a Galilean, tired of people trying to turn your home into someone else's kingdom. Now, hear Jesus describe His Kingdom.

Blessed are the poor in spirit, for theirs is the Kingdom of Heaven.

MATTHEW 5:3

Blessed are the meek, for they will inherit the earth.

MATTHEW 5:5

So do not worry, saying, "What shall we eat?" or "What shall we drink?" or "What shall we wear?" For the pagans run after all these things, and your heavenly Father knows that you need them. But seek first His Kingdom and His righteousness, and all these things will be given to you as well.

MATTHEW 6:31–33

Being asked by the Pharisees when the Kingdom of God would come, He answered them, "The Kingdom of God is not coming in ways that can be observed, nor will they say, 'Look, here it is!' or 'There!' for behold, the Kingdom of God is in the midst of you."

LUKE 17:20–21

The kingdom Jesus had in mind was like nothing the people of Galilee were used to. First introduced to the public as the Lamb of God who takes away the sin of the world (John 1:29, 36), Jesus' identity was that of a man of peace. His mission: to love the world into the Kingdom of God.

Is it possible for a kingdom built on a foundation of love to overcome a kingdom built by violent means? Can the peaceful Kingdom of God possibly compete with the brute force of the kingdom of men? After all, Jesus was crucified and the disciples were persecuted. During the first three centuries of the church, Christians were barely tolerated at best, violently persecuted at worst. Indeed, there are times when it appears the kingdoms of this world have the upper hand.

Desiring to get our way by our own effort instead of trusting God's way is, of course, a great temptation. The church at Corinth, for example, resorted to lawsuits as a form of conflict resolution. When the apostle Paul found out about this practice, he did more than to suggest they iron out their own disputes. He called on the Christians to do something absolutely contrary to the ways of the world.

To have lawsuits at all with one another is already a defeat for you.
Why not rather suffer wrong? Why not rather be defrauded? But you
yourselves wrong and defraud—even your own brothers!

1 CORINTHIANS 6:7-8

There is a natural resistance to doing things God's way. Letting yourself be wronged, as Paul suggested, does not exactly sound like a better solution than to take a brother to court. It is perhaps for this reason that God gives us the final chapter: how the kingdom based on love will fare when pitted against the kingdoms of the world:

And the ten horns that you saw are ten kings who have not yet received
royal power, but they are to receive authority as kings for one hour,
together with the beast. These are of one mind, and they hand over
their power and authority to the beast. They will make war on the
Lamb, and the Lamb will conquer them, for He is Lord of lords and
King of kings, and those with Him are called and chosen and faithful.

REVELATION 17:12-14

MAGDALA

MARY MAGDALENE'S FISHING VILLAGE

You know how to interpret the appearance of the sky, but you
cannot interpret the signs of the times.

MATTHEW 16:3

BACKGROUND, ARCHAEOLOGY, AND SIGNIFICANCE

BACKGROUND

The orchards and fields of Moshav Migdal now cover much of the area that was once the thriving town of Magdala. East of the main road, you will notice an area enclosed by a high wall containing mostly third-century A.D. houses; west of the road, dug into the rock, is part of the ancient cemetery. Much of the rest of the town, including the city of Jesus' day, is underwater. Since the level of the Sea of Galilee has changed over the centuries, many of the the piers, warehouses, and markets are submerged.

THE HISTORY OF MAGDALA

Magdala, the hometown of Mary Magdalene (or "Mary of Magdala"), was a fishing village nestled between the sheer cliffs of Mount Arbel and the Sea of Galilee. This prosperous town was known by other names as well. Migdal Nunia (Talmud, Pesahim 46a). Magadan (Matthew 15:39) and Dalmanutha (Mark 8:10) are also likely to be identified with ancient Magdala. The ancient Jewish historian Josephus knew the town as Taricheae from the Greek word meaning "fish pickling." In fact, one of the town's primary industries was the curing of fish for export to distant markets. Strabo, the Greek geographer, remarked "at the place called Taricheae, the lake supplies excellent fish for pickling" (Strabo, Geography 16.2.45).

Since the shore slopes gently to the sea at this point, Magdala was an ideal fishing town, once containing as many as 230 fishing boats. The town owed its prosperity, however, not only to the fishing industry, but also to the agricultural surplus of the surrounding area. The fertile plain extending northward from Magdala was referred to as Gennesaret in Jesus' day (Matthew 14:34).

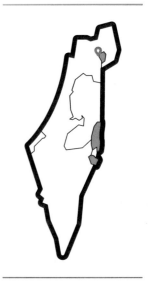

REFERENCES

Matthew 15:39–16:4

Matthew 27:56, 61

Mark 8:10–13

Mark 15:40–41, 47

Mark 16:9

Luke 8:2

John 20:1, 18

The fertile soil of the plain, along with the abundant water supply and mild climate, made the area extremely productive.

As early as the first century B.C., Magdala became a hotbed of anti-Roman sentiment. In about 54 B.C., the Romans put down a rebellion there, selling 30,000 residents as slaves (Josephus, Jewish War 1.8). Magdala was eventually resettled, and by A.D. 67, it could boast a population of 40,000 people and such urban amenities as a stadium, synagogue, hippodrome, and defensive walls.

JESUS IN MAGDALA

After a full day of teaching and feeding 4,000 people on the eastern shore, Jesus sailed west across the Sea of Galilee to Magdala. His miraculous powers had already attracted the attention of people looking for a leader, perhaps of yet another revolt against the Romans. However, when the leaders demanded a sign from Heaven, Jesus responded that no sign would be given to them except the sign of Jonah, referring to the three days He would spend in the grave (Matthew 15:39–16:4; Mark 8:10–13).

At first glance, it may appear that Jesus' ministry in Magdala had no lasting impact, but His most loyal follower, Mary of Magdala, was at Jesus' crucifixion (Matthew 27:56). She was also the first to see her resurrected Lord (Matthew 28:1).

THE FIRST REVOLT

A generation after Jesus, Magdala was again a rebel center in the First Revolt against Rome (66–73 A.D.) and the site of one of the bloodiest battles of the war. As Roman troops stormed the city, many of the rebels took to their boats. In the naval battle that ensued, the Romans massacred the Jews, destroying their boats and killing those who escaped into the water. Josephus reported:

A fearful sight met the eyes—the entire lake stained with blood and crammed with corpses; for there was not a single survivor. (Josephus, Jewish War 3.10)

Finally, the Romans rounded up the remaining insurgents hiding in the town. Pretending at first to release them, the Romans later captured them again down the road at Tiberias. Most of them were sold as slaves.

THE ARCHAEOLOGY OF MAGDALA

In 1960, archaeologists discovered the remains of first-century Magdala. To their surprise, the ruins were underwater. It is now known that most ancient harbors and waterfronts on the Sea of Galilee are submerged because of the change in water level.

The portions of the city dating from the third and fourth centuries A.D. are on land. In the early 1970s, the Franciscan order excavated this area, which included streets, houses, and a marketplace. A few ruins also date from the first century: a mosaic tile floor, depicting a fishing scene, is now on display in nearby Capernaum.

In January 1986, an exciting discovery was made when the water level of the Sea of Galilee was low after years of drought. Two brothers, from the local kibbutz found the outline of a boat in the mud. When the site was excavated, the find was determined to be a fishing boat from the first century.

Now preserved in a special chemical solution, the so-called "Jesus boat" may be seen in the museum at Kibbutz Ginnosar on the site of ancient Magdala. It is possible this was one of the boats sunk by the Romans on that fateful day during the First Revolt.

WHAT CAN WE LEARN FROM MAGDALA?

THE SIGN OF JONAH

> *And after sending away the crowds, He got into the boat and went to the region of Magadan. And the Pharisees and Sadducees came, and to test Him they asked Him to show them a sign from Heaven. He answered them, "When it is evening, you say, 'It will be fair weather, for the sky is red.' And in the morning, 'It will be stormy today, for the sky is red and threatening.' You know how to interpret the appearance of the sky, but you cannot interpret the signs of the times. An evil and adulterous generation seeks for a sign, but no sign will be given to it except the sign of Jonah." So He left them and departed.*
>
> MATTHEW 15:39–16:4

Some of the leaders in Magdala asked Jesus for a sign that He was who He claimed. What kind of "sign from Heaven" were they seeking? Jesus performed "signs" all over the region as well-known miracles. In fact, when another group of people, the disciples of John the Baptist, asked Jesus for a sign, this was the answer He gave them:

And Jesus answered them, "Go and tell John what you hear and see:
the blind receive their sight and the lame walk, lepers are cleansed
and the deaf hear, and the dead are raised up, and the poor have Good
News preached to them.
And blessed is the one who is not offended by Me."

MATTHEW 11:4–6

According to Jesus, then, the "sign" that He was the Son of God was the miracles that He performed. What more proof could He offer to the skeptics? Just a few hours before, when He was confronted in Magdala, Jesus had fed 4,000 people from a few loaves and fishes. Is it possible that this and other miracles were not enough to convince those who were asking Jesus for a sign?

The problem of Magdala, and of other recipients of Jesus' preaching, was people refusing to believe, even though they saw many signs:

For as Jonah became a sign to the people of Nineveh, so will the Son of
Man be to this generation. The queen of the South will rise up at the
judgment with the men of this generation and condemn them, for she
came from the ends of the earth to hear the wisdom of Solomon, and
behold, something greater than Solomon is here. The men of Nineveh
will rise up at the judgment with this generation and condemn it, for
they repented at the preaching of Jonah, and behold, something greater
than Jonah is here.

LUKE 11:30–32

Even the Israelites' ancient enemies, the Ninevites, believed when they heard a simple message from Jonah the prophet. Jesus, the One greater than Jonah, was now among the people of Magdala, and they did not believe His message.

Perhaps, the residents of Magdala wanted to experience God's power on their own terms. Having suffered before under the Romans, Magdala was a place where political dissenters thrived. The older people of Jesus' day would have had painful memories of Herod's brutality at the cliffs of Arbel (reference the Mount Arbel chapter). Perhaps, the "sign" the leaders were looking for was the credentials of a rebel leader. That role was never part of Jesus' mission.

We often want to experience God's power on our own terms. Magdala serves as a reminder of how, sometimes, we want more proof of God's existence... or His goodness... or His power. The signs He offered in the past are not enough for us here and now. For those who experienced God's kindness in various ways in the past, the distress of a present crisis may be overwhelming. We forget that God hasn't changed, that He is still as powerful and as good as He was before. Yet, we want another sign: if only God will do what we want, we will believe.

God already gave the ultimate sign: the resurrection of His Son Jesus from the dead.

> *For just as Jonah was three days and three nights in the belly of the great fish, so will the Son of Man be three days and three nights in the heart of the earth.*
>
> MATTHEW 12:40

God is trustworthy, and we can trust that demonstration of His power more than any evidence we could want. And, according to the apostle Paul, the power of that Sign is available for us today:

> *...having the eyes of your hearts enlightened, that you may know what is the hope to which He has called you, what are the riches of His glorious inheritance in the saints, and what is the immeasurable greatness of His power toward us who believe, according to the working of His great might that He worked in Christ when He raised Him from the dead and seated Him at His right hand in the heavenly places.*
>
> EPHESIANS 1:18–20

MT. CARMEL

BATTLEGROUND OF THE GODS

The Splendor of Carmel and Sharon; they will see the glory of the
LORD, the splendor of our God.

BACKGROUND, ARCHAEOLOGY AND SIGNIFICANCE

BACKGROUND

Although "Carmel" means "vineyard (or garden) of the Lord," the rocky and sparsely forested ascent from the east hardly reveals what this mountain looked like in Biblical times, when it was noted for its abundance of vegetation. The breeze from the Mediterranean brings dew and rain to the slopes of the mountain. On the eastern slopes, you may notice Bedouin tents and their flocks.

On the way to the summit sits a church commemorating the contest between Elijah and the prophets of Baal (1 Kings 18). Standing on the roof of this church, looking out for miles all around, it's easy to understand why this would have been the ideal site for such a contest. While there is a statue of Elijah outside the church, there are no physical remnants of the story in 1 Kings 18.

MOUNT CARMEL IN HISTORY

The mountain jutting out into the Mediterranean Sea attracted the attention of early Egyptian scribes, who called it "the gazelle's nose." Rather than a single peak, Mount Carmel actually consists of a range of mountains over 15 miles long. The Egyptians considered the mountain a military obstacle, since its three narrow passes could prove dangerous to armies attempting to march through.

Mount Carmel was the southern border of the area allotted to the tribe of Asher. Although the area was included in the allotment of Israelite tribes, it was not conquered until the reign of King David. In 1 Kings 9:13, Solomon gave away the cities of the territory of Asher to Hiram, king of Tyre. It was thus here that Jehu, King of Israel

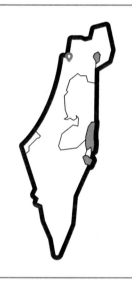

REFERENCES

Joshua 12:22

1 Kings 18:1 19:4

Song of Solomon 7:5

Jeremiah 46:18; 50:19

Nahum 1:4

Joshua 19:26

2 Kings 2:25; 4:25

Isaiah 35:2, 33:9

Amos 1:2

to the south, and the king of Tyre to the north presented their payment of tribute to the Assyrian King Shalmaneser III. The Assyrians eventually conquered the entire area in the eighth century B.C.

The mountain continued to be a religious site for centuries. In the fourth century BC, the Greeks built a temple to Zeus there, and the area continued as a shrine through the Roman period.

THE ARCHAEOLOGY OF MOUNT CARMEL

Excavations have been conducted in numerous caves on Mount Carmel. These caves show that early inhabitants took advantage of the area's fertility. Good hunting and wild grains attracted the earliest settlers. Mount Carmel never supported large settlements since transportation would have been difficult. No traces have been found of Carmel's ancient structures, such as the temple to Zeus. They may exist under the modern structures at Muhraqa or Haifa, the buildings located at the top of this mountain.

WHAT CAN WE LEARN FROM MOUNT CARMEL?

The people of Israel were commanded: "Fear the Lord your God, serve him only" (Deuteronomy 6:13). So, why were the people drawn away to worship the god Baal? After all, the contest on Mount Carmel was not between Israel and a rival nation, but between a lone prophet of the Lord and the Israelite prophets of Baal. Why did the Israelites follow a god who was not their own but was a Canaanite god?

The more we understand about Baal worship, the more meaningful the narrative of 1 Kings 18 becomes. Baal was the god of storms as well as fertility. It was to Baal that people would pray for good crops, rain, and increases in their flocks and families.

The people thought they had found a better source of rain in Baal. God took up the challenge by withholding the rain and the dew. In this way, the Lord set up the terms of the contest long before Elijah arrived. It was after three years of drought that Elijah challenged the prophets of Baal.

The Israelites found they were trying to fulfill a legitimate end by worshiping a false god. What they failed to recognize is that only the Lord is the giver of all good things, as James made clear many centuries later:

> *"Every good and perfect gift is from above, coming down from the Father of the heavenly lights, who does not change like shifting shadows."*

So we must ask, what legitimate needs are we trying to fulfill by looking to sources other than the Lord? God knows our every need, and He is more than willing to meet them:

> *"But seek first His kingdom and His righteousness, and all these things will be given to you as well."*

MATTHEW 6:33

In the language of Jesus, the word for "master" was "Baal". It is up to us to decide whether or not to trust God with our needs rather than allowing them to "master" us.

There is a powerful line in 1 Kings 18:21 when Elijah asks the people of Israel, "How long will you go limping between two different options?" We should ask ourselves the same question. How long will we go on limping between our sin and distractions versus being totally devoted to God?

In that story in 1 Kings 18, we see an example of such total devotion to God. A man named Obadiah risked his life because of his devotion to the Lord. It is only a side note in the story, but Obadiah's commitment is something worth remembering.

> *"Now Obadiah feared the Lord greatly, and when Jezebel cut off the prophets of the Lord, Obadiah took a hundred prophets and hid them by fifties in a cave and fed them with bread and water."*

1 KINGS 18: 3-4

This was a courageous move on Obadiah's part. He knew he would have been killed if caught, but he risked his life to care for God's people. Let us consider this type of devotion as we answer Elijah's question in the context of our own lives. How long will you go on limping? As Elijah stated in response to his own question in verse 21, "If the Lord is God, follow him."

CAESAREA MARATIMA

AN INTERNATIONAL PORT FOR THE SPREADING OF THE GOSPEL

On the next day we departed and came to Caesarea, and we entered the house of Philip the evangelist, who was one of the seven, and stayed with him.

ACTS 21:8

BACKGROUND, ARCHAEOLOGY, AND SIGNIFICANCE

As visitors drive along miles of sand dunes and scrub brush, most are unaware they have already arrived in Caesarea. Beneath the dunes are the houses of Israel's most populous city at the time of the early Church.

Your first glimpse of an excavated building will be the Roman Theatre. As you wander down the limestone streets toward what was once the third-largest port city in the entire Roman Empire, you will notice the Crusader walls and dry moat around the fortress.

Approaching the harbor, the beach may seem tiny. However, the bay to the north of the Crusader citadel forms only a small part of what was Herod's harbor, which was actually much larger. The original Roman harbor was actually a third of a mile off shore and has long since been covered by the sea.

One of the most impressive sights in Caesarea is the aqueduct. These graceful arches represent the city's lifeline, the water supply from Mount Carmel. Some of the arches are partially buried by sand and others have disappeared altogether as the sea claimed part of the original shoreline.

All that is visible of the former Roman capital of Judea are the relatively small areas that have been excavated. These areas provide small windows into Herod's once glorious port city.

THE HISTORY OF CAESAREA

Although Herod the Great founded many cities, he dedicated this city, his crowning architectural triumph, to his friend and patron Caesar Augustus. Herod received the coastal area in 30 B.C., which was previously gifted to Cleopatra by

QUICK FACTS

Caesarea Maritima was the third-largest port city in the Roman Empire.

It was the former Roman capital of Judea.

Herod the Great's Architectural Triumph.

The site of the first Gentile conversion to Christianity.

REFERENCES

Acts 8:40,

Acts 9:30,

Acts 10:1–48,

Acts 12:19b–23

Acts 18:22,

Acts 21:8–16,

Acts 23:23–27:1

Mark Antony. According to the Jewish historian Josephus, the site had previously been a small Sidonian trading post.

Herod began construction in 22 B.C. and inaugurated the magnificent new city 12 years later. Caesarea was the official capital of Judea for nearly 600 years after Herod's death. Roman procurators, such as Pontius Pilate, ruled Judaea from this city. Caesarea was the center of civic functions, such as the local courts, troop recruiting and housing, mints, and tax collection.

Jews and Gentiles populated Caesarea, although it was predominantly Gentiles, during the New Testament period. Tensions between the two groups ran high, sometimes to the point of bloodshed.

The Muslims captured Caesarea in 639 A.D., ruling it until the arrival of the Crusaders 460 years later. The Crusaders attempted to hold the area, fortifying it with the moat and towers you see today, but were expelled in 1265 A.D. The city was turned into a heap of ruins in 1291 A.D. and continued in that state until a small colony of Muslims from Bosnia settled there in 1878. Five years prior to the establishment of that colony, the Palestine Exploration Fund surveyed the area, thus beginning the archaeological interest in the site, which continues to this day.

The city layout has gradually been uncovered over the past century. The plan included streets, civic buildings, temples, sewer and water supply systems, warehouse vaults, and all entertainment centers (theatre, amphitheater, hippodrome, and baths) that were found in most Roman cities.

The Roman theatre is about 300 feet in diameter and would have accommodated 4,000 people. It was originally built by Herod, but was repaired and renovated over the 400 years in use. It was in this theatre that Herod Agrippa I was stricken with a disease as recorded in Acts 12:19–23.

Just before entering the area enclosed by the Crusader walls, you will see the warehouse area, containing as many as 100 vaults constructed during the Herodian period. Twenty vaults were built on each city block. Each vault is 96 feet long, 16 feet wide, and 15 feet high.

One of the most impressive buildings in Caesarea would have been the temple Herod built to the goddess of Rome. The temple included a colossal statue of Caesar, which according to Josephus, compared to the statue of Zeus, one of the eight wonders of the ancient world.

Archaeologists have found what they believe is the platform on which the temple was built. Like the Temple Mount in Jerusalem, Herod built a broad platform of imported white marble (supported by arches) on which to place the temple itself.

THE ARCHAEOLOGY OF CAESAREA

All that remains of the Caesarea temple are the ruins of the monumental staircase, which led from the lower level of the city to the temple platform. During the sixth century A.D., a church was built over the area where the temple to Rome stood. A massive marble foot found during the excavations may belong to the statue of Caesar described by Josephus. This foot is on display in the area outside the theatre.

One of the engineering problems Herod faced in building Caesarea was the water supply. There is no fresh water in the area, so it had to be carried a considerable distance using an aqueduct. The aqueduct built by Herod brought water from a spring at the foot of Mount Carmel. By the second century A.D., this water supply proved to be inadequate, and a second channel was added. This second channel brought water from a collection tunnel ten miles east of Caesarea and joined the original channel at the foot of Mount Carmel. In the fifth century, a second aqueduct was added. Near the aqueducts lie the ruins of synagogues from the Roman and Byzantine periods.

Philip was the first Christian to preach the Gospel to the people at Caesarea (Acts 8:40). For those disciples who received the Great Commission to preach the Gospel to "the uttermost parts of the earth," Caesarea qualified as such a place. We know nothing of the results of Philip's preaching there since the narrative of Acts shifts to the story of Paul's conversion.

Cornelius, a centurion in the Italian Regiment, was assigned to duty in Caesarea. He and his family were "devout and God-fearing" (Acts 10:2), giving to the needs of the poor and praying to God. He received a vision that he should send men to Joppa to bring back Simon Peter.

The next event that takes place in Caesarea is connected with the persecution of Peter and other Christian leaders in the church at Jerusalem. When Peter miraculously escaped from prison in Jerusalem, Herod Agrippa I executed the guards for allowing their prisoner to escape. Herod Agrippa I then went to Caesarea where he died in the theatre after accepting worship as a god, as Acts 12:19b–23 relates.

Paul is the next New Testament person to come to Caesarea, first as a visitor to stay with Philip. Later, he came as a prisoner awaiting trial. It was here that Paul appeared before Felix and then Portius Festus between 57 A.D. and 59 A.D. Paul used his right, as a Roman citizen, to appeal his case directly to Caesar. While waiting to be transferred to Rome, Paul shared the Gospel with Herod Agrippa II and Bernice, who rejected his message. Our last glimpse of Caesarea in the New Testament is of Paul leaving by ship to go to Rome.

WHAT CAN WE LEARN FROM CAESAREA?

> *And he said to them, "You yourselves know how unlawful it is for a Jew to associate with or to visit anyone of another nation, but God has shown me that I should not call any person common or unclean."*

ACTS 10:28

The conversion of Cornelius, the first Gentile Christian, was a dramatic turning point in the history of Christianity. Up to this point, the church was exclusively Jewish. Some of these early Jewish believers were from the Greek-speaking world, but most were from Galilee and Judea.

The importance of this event cannot be ignored. Luke's narrative of Cornelius' conversion is important enough that it is recorded twice in the book of Acts: once as the story occurred, and again as Peter related the story when confronted by his brothers in Jerusalem.

God's choice of Caesarea is a fitting monument to this great turning point in Christianity. As related in Acts, the story is not about the conversion of just any Gentile, but an officer in the hated Roman occupying forces. This officer lived not in just any city, but in the most pagan city in the country, the illegitimate capital of Palestine. He lived in a city located on Jewish soil dedicated to Caesar Augustus and to the worship of Rome. Not only were Gentiles to be included within the covenant of God's people, but such inclusion also transcended political boundaries.

Caesarea provides a lesson in divine irony: God chose a city of Jewish-Gentile conflict to be the launching point to unite all people, Jew and Gentile. He chose the city of Gentile 'impurity' to demonstrate that all who embrace Him are pure. He chose a city brimming with rejection to show that all are accepted under the same Gospel:

And He came and preached peace to you who were far off and peace
to those who were near. For through Him we both have access in one
Spirit to the Father.

EPHESIANS 2:17–18

Let us remember that we were once strangers to God's covenant. It is by grace alone that we were admitted into relationship with Him through Christ. Paul, grasping this truth, described it as the mystery of the Gospel:

When you read this, you can perceive my insight into the mystery
of Christ, which was not made known to the sons of men in other
generations as it has now been revealed to His holy apostles and
prophets by the Spirit. This mystery is that the Gentiles are fellow
heirs, members of the same body, and partakers of the promise in
Christ Jesus through the Gospel.

EPHESIANS 3:4–6

JOPPA

THE MERCY OF GOD IS RELENTLESS

But Jonah rose to flee to Tarshish from the presence of the Lord.
He went down to Joppa and found a ship going to Tarshish.
So he paid the fare and went down into it, to go with them to
Tarshish, away from the presence of the Lord.

JONAH 1:3

BACKGROUND, ARCHAEOLOGY, AND SIGNIFICANCE:

Joppa (Tel Aviv) is the southern end of the city. When you visit Israel today, you will fly into Tel Aviv, the major transportation hub people and goods in Israel. This also would have been true in ancient days, although you would have arrived by boat, rather than plane. The port of Joppa was of great significance in both the Old and New Testament because of the access it gave to Jerusalem and other sites in Israel. This would have been the port Herod the Great used to bring in materials for Caesarea Maritima in 10 B.C., approximately 30 miles to the north on the shore.

There is a Tel (mound) located in Jaffa, called Tel Yafo, which is over 130 feet tall. This site would have provided a perfect view of the coastline, which was important for past military purposes. Archeology shows us the natural port of Jaffa has been used since the Bronze Age.

JOPPA IN THE OLD TESTAMENT

Biblically speaking, Joppa is referenced in Joshua 19:46 in the context of an inheritance for the tribe of Dan after the conquests of Israel. Most likely, this port city was not under Israelite control until the conquest of David. Solomon, David's son, used the main port of Joppa for importing cedars on rafts from Lebanon to build the first temple (2 Chronicles 2:15–16). Then 800 years later, this port was used again to import material for the rebuilding of the Temple (Ezra 3:7). This speaks to the significance of Joppa over hundreds of years.

Perhaps one of the most well known stories in the Bible that takes place in Joppa is Jonah's struggle with God. God clearly told Jonah to go to Nineveh, located in the east, which was in the Babylon kingdom (modern day Iraq). Jonah was commissioned to prophesy to the people of Nineveh concerning their ungodliness (Jonah

QUICK FACTS

This city is the oldest part of Tel Aviv and has always been a port city.

It is called "Joppa" in the Old Testament and can be referred to as "Yafo."

This port was used to import materials for the building of both Temples.

This is the port where Jonah went to flee from the presence of God.

REFERENCES

Joshua 19:46

2 Chronicles 2:16

Ezra 3:7

Jonah 1:3–4

Acts 9:36–43

Acts 10:9–23

1:3). They were evil people and enemies of Jonah and his people. Instead of obeying God, Jonah headed to Joppa to find the first ship he could board to get away from the presence and commands of God. He paid a fare and caught a ship headed west, and the rest of the story is history. It is an easy conclusion to draw that God placed Jonah back near this port once the large fish spit him out onto dry land.

JOPPA IN THE NEW TESTAMENT

After the death of Christ, we are told of a few more events that took place in Joppa. The New Testament account of Peter's resurrection of the widow Tabitha (Dorcas in Greek) takes place in Joppa as written in Acts 9:36–42. Also, in Acts 10:10–23, while Peter was in Joppa, we are told he experienced a vision of a large sheet filled with 'clean' and 'unclean' animals being lowered from Heaven, together with a message from the Holy Spirit to accompany several messengers to Cornelius in Caesarea. Therefore, we can conclude that the early Church had a presence in this city.

There are other stories and accounts of great Jewish and Roman history taking place in Joppa. We know that, in the 700s B.C., Hezekiah ruled over this city and fought against Sennacherib to keep its control. In the 300s B.C., Alexander the Great's troops were stationed in Joppa. It later became a Seleucid Hellenized port until it was taken over by the Maccabean rebels (1 Maccabees x.76, xiv.5) and the re-founded Jewish kingdom.

During the Roman repression of the Jewish Revolt in the first century A.D., Joppa was captured and burned by Cestius Gallus. The Roman Jewish historian Josephus writes that 8,400 inhabitants were massacred (Jewish War 2.507–509, 3:414–426). Pirates, operating from the rebuilt port, incurred the wrath of Vespasian, who destroyed the city and erected a citadel in its place, installing a Roman garrison there.

Archaeological excavations of Tel Yafo have yielded at least seven layers of occupational levels, dating back to the seventeenth century B.C. This is not an easy place to excavate because there are many people still living and using this small Tel Aviv suburb every day. While large boats no longer use the port, it is still a hub for all sorts of small aquatic vessels.

WHAT CAN WE LEARN FROM JOPPA?

Has God ever been clear with you about something, yet you chose to ignore Him?

Perhaps God told you to reconcile a relationship, care for someone who is hurting, or share the Gospel with someone who doesn't know Jesus.

Maybe you heard His voice, but you chose to ignore it and run the other way. That is exactly what Jonah did.

WHO WAS JONAH?

Jonah (meaning "dove") was a prophet who lived in the eighth or ninth century B.C. during the reign of King Jeroboam II (782–753 BC) according to 1 Kings 17:7–24. Many times, in the Old Testament, we see a strong correlation between a person's name and their demeanor. Therefore, it may be safe to assume that Jonah was a gentle and non-confrontational man who tried to avoid conflict at all cost. Many theologians and commentators refer to him as the "reluctant prophet" because of the way he avoided God's command in the book bearing his name.

We know Jonah's birth place was Gath-hepher in Northern Israel because it is mentioned in 2 Kings:

> *He restored the border of Israel from Lebo-hamath as far as the Sea*
> *of the Arabah, according to the Word of the LORD, the God of Israel,*
> *which He spoke by His servant Jonah the son of Amittai, the prophet,*
> *who was from Gath-hepher.*
>
> ## 2 KINGS 14:25

 It is interesting to note that his father's name Amittai means "truth," which adds significance to the call of Jonah's life to speak the truth on behalf of God. Many believe that he was also the son of his later-widowed mother Zarephath.

Before Jonah was ever born, God knew exactly how He would use Jonah. God even knew Jonah would struggle when commanded to go to Nineveh. However, we can learn from Jonah's life that God knows our credentials and qualms, but He chooses to use us anyway. God's sovereignty will always prevail, even over our preferences. We see several times, in the book of Jonah, that "God made" or "God appointed" the storm to appear, the fish to swallow Jonah, and even the worm to eat the plant at the end of the book of Jonah. There's no denying God was completely in control of what was happening throughout the story, even though Jonah tried everything in his power to stop.

It should be a comfort to know there is a God who is in control of our mistakes and sins; He is masterful at weaving them into His perfect plan.

When Jonah came to Joppa, his intention was to get away from the Lord. In Jonah 1:3, we are told that he "paid the price" to jump on a ship headed to Tarshish. The truth for our life is that there is always going to be a ship headed in the wrong direction. This begs the question: will you pay the price to try to get away from the commands of God in your life or will you stay the course? Eugene Peterson pointed out in his aptly titled book that our call, as Christians, is to live a life of A Long Obedience in the Same Direction. We should always avoid any opportunity to head the wrong direction when it comes to living a life of faithfulness to God.

HEAR HIS VOICE AND DO NOT RUN

God spoke to Jonah without a hiccup or stutter, but Jonah didn't like what God had to say. Hebrews says that

> *In the past [God] spoke through prophets... But in these days He has spoken to us by His Son whom He appointed over all things."*
>
> HEBREWS 1:1-2

Jesus gave us a clear way to live. The Holy Spirit applies this truth to our lives daily, but the choice is ours as to whether we will listen and obey. Sure, there are bound to be things we don't want to do or things about which we wish we could change God's mind. However, we are not God, nor do we have His view on the greater picture or purposes. Our calling is to trust God through faith and obey Him with our actions.

> *"Today if you hear His voice, do not harden your hearts."*
>
> HEBREWS 3:7-8

NAZARETH

THE HOME OF JESUS ON EARTH

Coming to His hometown, He began teaching the people in their
synagogue, and they were amazed.

MATTHEW 13:54

BACKGROUND, ARCHAEOLOGY, AND SIGNIFICANCE:

Today, Nazareth is a bustling city, swarming with activity around the Basilica of the Annunciation. It doesn't seem to fit our mental picture of the little village where Jesus grew up. As we learn more about the history of this area, we realize Nazareth wasn't the obscure locale we thought it to be.

Nazareth is next to one of the most important roads that traveled through Israel. The city is nestled in the middle of a bowl-like depression of white limestone hills. As you walk the winding streets, it may be helpful to remember that in Jesus' day, the town extended from where the Basilica of the Annunciation stands now to where St. Gabriel's Church is today. It was from one of those surrounding limestone hills that the towns-people tried to throw Jesus off a cliff (Luke 4:29).

Visitors have a panoramic view of the north-eastern part of the Jezreel Valley from the top of these hills that form the Nazareth Ridge. These hillsides have witnessed the battles of Deborah and Barak against Sisera and the Canaanites from Hazor (Judges 4–5). It was also here that Elijah raised the widow's son from the dead at Shunem (2 Kings 4:32–35). Jesus similarly raised a widow's son nearby at Nain (Luke 7:11–15).

THE HISTORY OF NAZARETH

Although the name Nazareth is not found in the Old Testament, archaeological excavations prove there was at least a small settlement here prior to the time of the patriarchs in the third millennium B.C.

Two nearby towns are listed as part of the area allotted to the tribe of Zebulon. Japhia is just southwest of Nazareth and Gath Hepher is to the northeast of Nazareth. These two locations are

REFERENCES

Matthew 2:22–23; 13:53–58; 21:11

Mark 1:9, 24; 6:1–6; 14:67

Luke 1:26–38; 2:4, 39, 51; 4:15–30

John 1:45–46; 19:19

Acts 10:38

listed in Joshua 19:12–13. Gath Hepher is perhaps best known as the home of the prophet Jonah (2 Kings 14:25).

The area, like the rest of the Northern Kingdom, was depopulated following the Assyrian conquest of the eighth century B.C. Nazareth was resettled by 300 B.C. These newcomers may have been a clan from the family of King David, as both Mary and Joseph's lineages trace back to the royal family. The settlers could have come directly from their Babylonian exile. It is also possible they came from elsewhere in Judea, perhaps as part of the Hasmonean policy of resettling the Galilee with Jewish families.

The new inhabitants of this agricultural village dug into the soft limestone to make numerous cisterns for holding runoff water, as well as basements, grain silos, storage bins, and ritual baths. Nazareth remained a small town. Estimates of its population during the time of Jesus range from 150 to 480 people.

THE ARCHAEOLOGY OF NAZARETH

Archaeologists have discovered remains dating from the third millennium B.C. through the first millennium B.C., but not enough to suggest that it was continuously inhabited. The site was apparently not inhabited at all from about 700–300 B.C. In about 300 B.C., settlers moved here and established a village. The presence of tombs from this period marks the approximate town limits, which were about 3,000 feet by 650 feet in area.

Because there is only one good spring in Nazareth, it is certain where the well was from which Mary drew water. The spring is located half a mile north of the Basilica of the Annunciation in the Greek Orthodox Church of St. Gabriel.

Although the current St. Gabriel's church was built in the seventeenth century, it is built over the remains of three earlier churches. The church received its name because this is likely the site where Mary received the news from the archangel Gabriel that she would give birth to a son.

When the previous eighteenth century basilica was demolished to make way for the new one in 1955, the area below the church was excavated. A number of caves, grain silos, cisterns, and olive and wine presses were discovered, all carved out of the soft limestone.

Since some of the caves had walls in front of them, it was clear that they had been used as houses. Some cave-houses also had walls inside, dividing the living space into rooms. Records indicate that relatives of Jesus continued to live in Nazareth for two centuries after His death, so this church is quite possibly located over the home of Joseph and Mary.

The Church of St. Joseph (also known as the Church of the Carpenter Shop) is north of the Basilica of the Annunciation. Although it is said to be above the site of Joseph's carpentry shop, excavations have shown that the Crusader ruins below the church are actually built upon agricultural installations, namely a wine press and silo.

Another interesting archaeological note is the possible location of the synagogue in which Jesus taught and read. This synagogue was probably destroyed in A.D. 67 when the Romans put down the First Revolt. Records suggest that it was rebuilt, and there are two possible locations. One is the Church of the United Greeks. While there are some inscriptions and Jewish symbols, there is no real archaeological evidence of an ancient synagogue here. A more likely site is the area of the Muslim cemetery near the marketplace of Nazareth. Excavations revealed remains of a Byzantine church on the site. Again, the continued presence of Jesus' family in Nazareth lends credence to the tradition.

NAZARETH IN THE NEW TESTAMENT

It was in the synagogue at Nazareth where Jesus stood to read from the book of Isaiah:

> *"The Spirit of the Lord is on Me, because He has anointed Me to preach Good News to the poor. He has sent Me to proclaim freedom for the prisoners and recovery of sight for the blind, to release the oppressed, to proclaim the year of the Lord's favor." Then He rolled up the scroll, gave it back to the attendant and sat down. The eyes of everyone in the synagogue were fastened on Him, and He began by saying to them, "Today this Scripture is fulfilled in your hearing."*

LUKE 4:18–22

The crowd complimented Jesus and apparently invited Him to perform miracles. Within minutes, however, the emotions of the crowd turned to hate when Jesus suggested that only Gentiles would listen to a prophet. They drove Jesus out of town, westward toward the brow of the hill, and attempted to throw Him off the cliff (Luke 4:29).

It is not known whether Jesus ever returned to Nazareth. His family continued to live there, and after the resurrection, they became leaders in the early church. After Jesus' brother James was martyred, his cousin Simeon succeeded him as head of the church in Jerusalem. Simeon was the son of Cleophas and Mary, Jesus' aunt on his mother's side (John 19:25).

Simeon was crucified for his faith at the age of 120. The strong connection of the church with Jesus' relatives in Nazareth continued for at least another 200 years.

SO WHAT CAN WE LEARN FROM NAZARETH?

JESUS THE BUILDER

In Jesus' day, Nazareth was a simple agricultural settlement. In such a small village, there would have been some trades or specialized occupations. There would have been a rabbi, tanners, shepherds, a potter, and builders. Many of these tradesmen would have farmed as well. It would have been necessary for most residents to make or supplement their living by tilling the soil. Typically, each family would have had a small plot for planting olive trees, grapevines, vegetables, and grain.

Some areas would have had carpenters to make doors and wooden furniture. But in Nazareth, a builder would have been a stonemason. The word "builder" is actually the correct translation of the Greek word "tekton."

This insight brings many verses to life when we reconsider the building activities of Joseph and possibly Jesus. Jesus frequently used building metaphors from His own experience to illustrate His lessons.

In the Sermon on the Mount, Jesus contrasted wise and foolish builders (Matthew 7:24–27). The wise builder dug deep to lay the foundation on rock. The foolish builder built without a foundation. When the storms of life struck the houses, only the well-built house remained intact.

Three of the Gospels record a message in which Jesus referred to Himself as the cornerstone, the most important stone in any building. It is the cornerstone that sets the horizontal and vertical planes for two sides of the building and the level of the entire structure.

The Old Testament makes it clear that the people were to look for a "cornerstone" to come from the tribe of Judah (Zechariah 10:4). Isaiah also describes this cornerstone:

See, I lay a stone in Zion, a tested stone, a precious cornerstone for a sure foundation; the one who trusts will never be dismayed. I will make justice the measuring line and righteousness the plumb line.

ISAIAH 28:16

Jesus described Himself as that very stone. As He quoted from the Scriptures, He identified Himself as the cornerstone laid by God. It is God, then, who laid the "cornerstone" of His Son. How fitting that both God the Father and God the Son are builders.

However, a cornerstone does not exist alone; it is the foundation of a building. The apostle Paul tells us about the building that Jesus supports:

> *"Consequently, you are no longer foreigners and aliens, but fellow citizens with God's people and members of God's household, built on the foundation of the apostles and prophets, with Christ Jesus Himself as the chief cornerstone. In Him the whole building is joined together and rises to become a holy temple in the Lord. And in Him you too are being built to become a dwelling in which God lives by His Spirit."*

EPHESIANS 2:19–22

Peter also used this metaphor:

> *"As you come to Him, the living Stone rejected by men but chosen by God and precious to Him, you also, like living stones, are being built into a spiritual house to be a holy priesthood, offering spiritual sacrifices acceptable to God through Jesus Christ."*

1 PETER 2:4–5

We are built upon the foundation stone of Christ. And as Christ's Church, we are not built to stand alone but together. We are built to be holy, like no other building. We are living stones, actively serving God.

When we become aligned with the Cornerstone, our lives will add to the reputation and glory of the Builder. When people see who we are, they should see what we represent. Our outward actions should reflect the inward work of God in our lives.

> *For we are God's masterpiece. He has created us anew in Christ Jesus, so we can do the good things He planned for us long ago.*

EPHESIANS 2:10

THE JEZREEL VALLEY

REAPING WHAT YOU SOW

Again the watchman reported, "He reached them, but he is not coming back. And the driving is like the driving of Jehu the son of Nimshi, for he drives furiously."

2 KINGS 9:20

BACKGROUND, ARCHAEOLOGY, AND SIGNIFICANCE

BACKGROUND

The Jezreel Valley will strike your eye with a kaleidoscope of shades of abundance—the gold of ripened grain, the brown of freshly plowed fields, the green of sprouting vegetables and fruit. The surrounding mountains are geographic parameters for the valley (in modern Hebrew, it is simply called "the valley").

The Jezreel Valley is a large area of land, running the entire width of the country. For this reason, your first glimpse of the valley may come from one of several places. It is visible from the top of Mount Carmel in the west, while from the cliffs of Arbel in the east, you can see Mount Tabor rising from the valley floor. Some of the passes into the valley are guarded by Megiddo and Beth Shean, from which you may also get your first glimpse of Jezreel. Standing on the Nazareth ridge, you may look to the south and get a panoramic view of the valley stretching from horizon to horizon.

Your first view of the valley will help you understand why it played such an important role in the history of the region. Its fertility, as well as its use as a thoroughfare, placed Jezreel in the pathway of farmers and soldiers alike.

THE GEOGRAPHY OF THE VALLEY

The Jezreel Valley has been known by a number of names in its history, including Esdraelon (its Greek name) and the valley of Megiddo or Armageddon. The valley is roughly in the shape of an arrow pointing toward the northwest. It is bordered by Mount Carmel on the southwest, Mount Gilboa on the southeast, Mount More on the east, the Nazareth ridge on the north, and the low hill country of Galilee on the northwest. The

QUICK FACTS

The Jezreel Valley is a site where the past and future prophetic battles are fought.

This valley runs the entire width of the land of Israel.

It is fertile but also the main passageway, making it a coveted piece of property throughout the Bible.

It is surrounded by significant geography, such as Mt. Tabor, Mt. Gilboa, and Ein Harod.

REFERENCES

Genesis 49:14

Joshua 17:11–16; 19:18

Judges 1:27–28; 6:33; 7:1, 12

1 Samuel 29:1

2 Samuel 2:9

1 Kings 4:12; 18:46; 21:1–24

2 Kings 9:10; 9:15–10:11

Hosea 1:4; 2:22–23

Revelation 16:16

valley owes its fertility to the abundant topsoil that is washed down from the surrounding hills.

George Adam Smith noted the relation of the valley to the entire region of Samaria:

Nature has manifestly set Esdraelon [the Greek name for Jezreel] in the arms of Samaria. Accordingly in Old Testament times they shared, for the most part, the same history; in tribal days, though Esdraelon was assigned to Zebulun and Issachar, Manasseh, the keeper of the hills to the south, claimed towns upon it; in the days of the kingdom, the chariots of Samarian kings, the feet of Samarian prophets, traversed Esdraelon from Carmel to Jordan. (The Historical Geography of the Holy Land, p.246)

Although the valley is noteworthy for its fertile land, its strategic value has made the name a watchword throughout history. The Jezreel Valley is the nexus of numerous connections to points north, east, south, and west. The international road from Egypt to Mesopotamia went through the Jezreel Valley; thus armies from the times of the pharaohs of Egypt to the British troops under General Allenby in World War I have tramped across its breadth. One entrance into the valley is from the Mediterranean Sea in the west along the foot of Mount Carmel, a route which Elijah the prophet ran in order to reach the palace of Ahab at the city of Jezreel. Other entrances into the valley include the passes through Mount Carmel—Jokneam, Megiddo, Taanach, and Jenin (near the biblical city of Dothan).

The entrance from the Jordan Valley is guarded by Beth Shean; it was through this entrance that the Midianites came with their camels in the time of Gideon. Travelers from the area of Galilee could also enter the valley through the Arbel Pass around Mount Tabor. The valley has become better known by its New Testament name.

And they assembled them at the place that in Hebrew is
called Armageddon.

REVELATION 16:16

Mark Twain imagined such a "gathering of the kings" throughout history:

The Plain of Esdraelon—"the battlefield of the nations"—only sets one
to dreaming of Joshua and Benhadad and Saul and Gideon; Tamerlane,
Tancred, Coeur de Lion, and Saladin; the warrior kings of Persia,
Egypt's heroes, and Napoleon—for they all fought here. If the magic
of the moonlight could summon from the graves of forgotten centuries

and many lands the countless myriads that have battled on this wide,
far-reaching floor, and array them in the thousand strange costumes of
their hundred nationalities, and send the vast host sweeping down the
plain, splendid with plumes and banners and glittering lances, I could
stay here an age to see the phantom pageant.[1]

THE JEZREEL VALLEY IN THE BIBLE

No area in the world has probably seen more action than this singularly important valley. Indeed, to narrate the history of the area is to narrate the history of the Middle East. The valley figures prominently in the early military campaigns of the Egyptian pharaohs. Joseph's brothers watched the slow progress of the trading caravan approach this valley from the east and sold him as a slave destined for Egypt. By the time the Israelites entered the land, the fortified cities of Taanach, Megiddo, Beth Shean, and Dothan—cities that guard the passes into the valley—were held by the Canaanites for centuries.

It is at Jezreel the armies of Deborah and Gideon defeated their foes, which came into the valley from the east. Philistines entered from the west to defeat the outnumbered Israelites, killing Saul and Jonathan. Solomon fortified the key city of Megiddo to control the pass most often used by invaders. King Ahab built the city of Jezreel in the valley as the site of his winter palace, protected as it was from western winds. Here, too, was the vineyard of Naboth, which was close to the palace of Ahab. It was here that Jehu killed Jezebel and the entire royal family.

The story of Naboth's vineyard is told in 1 Kings 21. King Ahab of Israel chose the site of Jezreel for his palace; as one would expect for such a fertile area, the area had fine vineyards. Naboth inherited one such vineyard close to the palace. When Ahab decided he wanted that particular vineyard, he asked Naboth to sell or trade it to him. Since giving (or trading) away what God had given to His ancestors was unthinkable, Naboth refused. Ahab returned to the palace and pouted, refusing to eat.

When Jezebel heard the reason for his sullenness, she chided him for not acting like a king. She, of course, was not an Israelite and was reflecting her own Phoenician cultural background in which all land was considered to be the king's. As far as Jezebel was concerned, what the king wanted, he received, and so her next action would have been acceptable in her home country. She sent out letters under King Ahab's seal asking the el-

....

1   Mark Twain, *The Innocents Abroad* (1869; repr. Pleasantville, NY: The Reader's Digest Association, 1990), pp. 336–7.

ders and nobles of the city to invite Naboth to a feast. There, Naboth was falsely accused and summarily killed, and Ahab had his vineyard. Where was justice at a time like this?

It remained for the leader Jehu to avenge the violence Jezebel brought on Naboth and many of the LORD's people. After killing King Joram, Jezebel's son, who had been recuperating from wounds received in a battle, Jehu set out to get Jezebel, who appeared with eye makeup and an elaborate hairdo—dressed to kill, one might say. It is with a smug, false sense of security that Jezebel looked out the window calling Jehu, his master's murderer. She obviously did not expect to be next. However, two officials betrayed Jezebel by throwing her out of the window where horses trampled her to death. When Jehu ordered for Jezebel to be buried, his servants reported they could find only her skull, feet, and hands. The dogs had eaten the rest.

WHAT CAN WE LEARN FROM THE JEZREEL VALLEY?

THE LAW OF THE HARVEST

The name "Jezreel" means "God sows." It is here, at Jezreel with the incident of Naboth's vineyard, that the principle of sowing and reaping can be dramatically seen.

As it is in agriculture, so it is in life; there is always an interval between sowing and reaping. For Jezebel, it would be years before she would suffer the consequences of her deeds. When faced by the prophet Elijah, King Ahab was repentant and was spared from witnessing the calamity that would engulf his entire family. For Jezebel, the very place where the dogs licked the blood of Naboth would be where dogs eventually ate Jezebel's body.

A long time passed between the commission of the crime and the passing of judgment. Elijah was no longer on the scene, and Ahab had already died of wounds received in a battle. It seemed everyone forgot about the Naboth incident—everyone, perhaps, but God. Consider this New Testament passage:

> Do not be deceived: God is not mocked, for whatever one sows, that
> will he also reap. For the one who sows to his own flesh will from the

flesh reap corruption, but the one who sows to the Spirit will from the
Spirit reap eternal life.

GALATIANS 6:7–8

Now think of that in relation to the Old Testament story and what happened here in the valley. There was nothing left of Jezebel except her skull, her hands, and feet. Why were these particular parts left? A passage from Proverbs may provide some clues:

There are six things that the LORD hates, seven that are an
abomination to Him: haughty eyes, a lying tongue, and hands that
shed innocent blood, a heart that devises wicked plans, feet that make
haste to run to evil, a false witness who breathes out lies, and one who
sows discord among brothers.

PROVERBS 6:16–19

Jezebel was guilty of all of these crimes, and her physical remains were a testimony to her treachery. God was not only passing judgment, but also illustrating the principle of the harvest. At Jezreel, Jezebel reaped what she sowed.

However, this principle has a positive side as well. The harvest is a time of joy, a time of gathering the fruit of one's labor. As God invested in us by sending His Son, so He rejoices when we reflect His generosity by giving ourselves to others. Paul used the metaphor of the harvest to teach that our own effectiveness for God depends upon our willingness to invest what God gives to us.

The point is this: whoever sows sparingly will also reap sparingly, and whoever sows bountifully will also reap bountifully. Each one must give as he has decided in his heart, not reluctantly or under compulsion, for God loves a cheerful giver. And God is able to make all grace abound to you, so that having all sufficiency in all things at all times, you may abound in every good work. As it is written,

"He has distributed freely, He has given to the poor; His righteousness
endures forever." He who supplies seed to the sower and bread for food
will supply and multiply Your seed for sowing and increase the harvest
of Your righteousness.

2 CORINTHIANS 9:6–10

MEGIDDO

STRONGHOLD OF THE VALLEY

The capturing of Megiddo is the capturing of a thousand towns!

THE ANNALS OF PHARAOH THUTMOSE III

BACKGROUND, ARCHAEOLOGY, AND SIGNIFICANCE

Megiddo was at first a Canaanite city, but the Egyptians were among the first and most formidable assailants of the city, most notably in 1468 B.C. during the reign of Thutmose III. Thutmose's forces besieged Megiddo for seven months after which the Egyptians seized and plundered the city, although presumably not for the first time. Toward the end of Egypt's dominance in the region, Megiddo was caught in the tumult of the revolt against Egypt.

During the far-reaching military exploits of the Assyrian King Tiglath-pileser III, Megiddo came under Assyrian control. Although the Assyrians are believed to have destroyed the city in the course of their conquest, it nonetheless became Tiglath-pileser's regional headquarters in Palestine, probably around 732 B.C. However, the city not fortified well in contrast to its earlier renditions under the Egyptians and the Israelites, and was destroyed again in 609 B.C., "perhaps by Pharaoh Neco." Megiddo was never again fortified and its inhabitants left for good in 350 B.C. during the reign of the Persian Empire.

THE GEOGRAPHY OF MEGIDDO

Megiddo has a long, violent, and tumultuous history, telling the story of the ebb and flow of empires and their influence in the Ancient Near East. The city sits at what was once a strategic crossroads of the Fertile Crescent, overlooking Wadi Arah, the primary passage through the Carmel mountain range on the south and east, as well as the Esdraelon plain, one of the most fertile agricultural breadbaskets in Palestine, on the east and north. The city's location at the juncture of these trade and travel routes gave its rulers a decided advantage in controlling the highway itself.

REFERENCES

Joshua 12:21; 17:11

Judges 1:27; 5:19

1 Kings 4:12; 9:15-19

2 Kings 9:27; 23:28-30

2 Chronicles 35:22

Zechariah 12:11

Revelation 16:12-16

THE HISTORY OF MEGIDDO

The first recorded battle in the area was a major engagement in 1,468 B.C. between the defending Canaanites and Egyptian troops under the leadership of Pharaoh Thutmose III. The Canaanites failed to guard the strategic Megiddo pass against the Egyptian advance, and Thutmose III took the city from a combined Canaanite force. The annals of Amenhotep II, a later pharaoh, describe Megiddo as an Egyptian base rather than a Canaanite city. Later records of Egyptian correspondence show Megiddo in alternate stages of rebellion and submission.

Under the Persians, Megiddo became a provincial capital but was abandoned by about 330 B.C. A Jewish settlement existed nearby until A.D. 120, when it was taken over by a legion of the Roman army. In Jesus' day, there were no inhabitants in the ancient city of Megiddo.

THE ARCHAEOLOGY OF MEGIDDO

Flint sickles found on the site reveal Megiddo's earliest inhabitants were farmers who harvested grain. Remains of "mud-brick houses," "rock-cut pits for storage,"[2] as well as other implements give archaeologists a rough picture of the lifestyle of Megiddo's first community.

Archaeological discoveries from sometime in the Early Bronze Age (3000-2000 B.C.) prove the city's transformation into a "major urban center." Among these findings are an impressive "sacred area," including at least four temples built over time, altars, including one altar standing at four and a half feet tall with a diameter of twenty-five feet, and the remains of animal sacrifices.[3] During the Bronze Age Megiddo was also fortified with walls, the largest of which was twenty-five feet thick and sixteen feet high. After the city's destruction at the end of the Bronze Age, signs point to Megiddo reduced to its villagelike origins for a time.

Some years later the Egyptians rebuilt the city's fortifications and once again transformed the city into a cosmopolitan hub, building a variety of housing units and several palaces. After losing control of Megiddo, the city was regained for Egypt by Thutmose III who destroyed the city and then rebuilt it in splendor, evidenced by the discovery of many luxurious items from this time, including jewelry, beads, gold, and some two hundred ivory carvings or plaques.

....

2   DeVries, *Cities of the Biblical World*, 218.

3   Ibid., 219.

After this era the city was again destroyed and remained in relative disrepair until rebuilt as a "fortified city" by Solomon.[4] Remains of palaces built by Solomon as well as a variety of Israelite "cult objects including horned altars, cylindrical pottery offering stands," and other artifacts from this period.[5] The influence of later Israelite kings, such as Ahab, include a redesigned city wall, stables, "storehouses," and an engineered "water system."[6]

MEGIDDO IN THE BIBLE

Joshua 12:21 lists the king of Megiddo as one of 31 kings defeated, although the city was apparently not occupied by the Israelites at that time. King David later conquered the strategic cities guarding the Jezreel Valley. Solomon included Megiddo in one of his administrative districts, which included Taanach and Beth Shean (1 Kings 4:12). He fortified the city along with Jerusalem, Hazor, and Gezer (1 Kings 9:15).

Egyptians destroyed the city during the reign of Solomon's son Rehoboam (1 Kings 14:25 and 2 Chronicles 12:4). Megiddo later became an important center in the Northern Kingdom after King Ahab rebuilt the city. Megiddo did not remain in Israelite control for long because the King of Aram attacked and destroyed Megiddo in 815 B.C. Megiddo was rebuilt during the reign of Jeroboam II, but this was the last period of its greatness. Tiglath-Pileser III, King of Assyria, took the city and made it a provincial capital in 722 B.C. During the next century, Pharoah Neco killed King Josiah of Judah at Megiddo (2 Kings 23:29).

WHAT CAN WE LEARN FROM MEGIDDO?

The violent history of Megiddo is sobering indeed. And yet it is here, before the ramparts of this troubled city, so often violently snatched back and forth between the grasping hands of hostile empires, that the Lord of Hosts Himself will win the final victory against the prince of this world. It is before Megiddo, whether as a literal or figurative location, that the grasping power of Satan will at last be vanquished before the resurrected Christ and His army.

It seems that in the story of Megiddo, past, present, and future, God underscores His promise to bring vengeance upon His enemies and vindicate His people. Neither the murderous raging of the nations nor the

---

4   Ibid., 221.

5   Ibid., 222.

6   Ibid.

violent schemes of the Devil himself can thwart God's power to secure ultimate victory. And, perhaps, the same principle can apply to the lives of those who belong to Christ.

No matter how many battles we think to have lost, no matter how many "sieges" we have endured, no matter how many times we have been throttled by the hands of the enemy, God secures the victory for us in Christ.

> *"And I heard a loud voice from the throne saying, "Behold, the dwelling place of God is with man. He will dwell with them, and they will be his people, and God himself will be with them as their God. He will wipe away every tear from their eyes, and death shall be no more, neither shall there be mourning, nor crying, nor pain anymore, for the former things have passed away."*

REVELATION 21:3-4

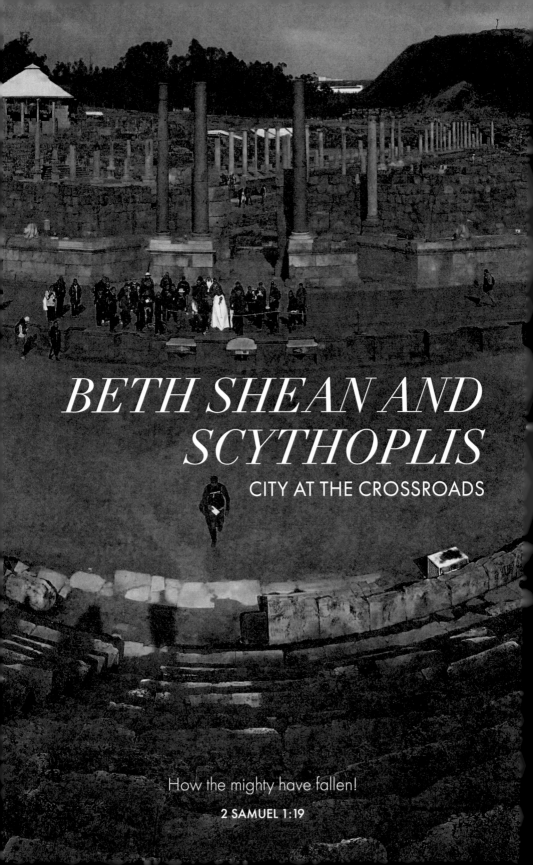

BETH SHEAN AND SCYTHOPLIS

CITY AT THE CROSSROADS

How the mighty have fallen!

2 SAMUEL 1:19

BACKGROUND, ARCHAEOLOGY, AND SIGNIFICANCE

The city of Beth Shean was an important economic and military center for thousands of years. Its strategic value comes from its location at the intersection of the Jordan and Jezreel Valleys, its control of a Jordan River ford, and its location near the main international road from Egypt.

THE GEOGRAPHY OF BETH SHEAN AND SCYTOPOLIS

Beth Shean was located at the intersection of the Jordan Valley and the Harod Valley, an extension of the Jezreel Valley. The Old Testament city is located beneath a very large tell. There is a commanding view of the two valleys from the top of the tel. In addition to its strategic location, fertile farmland and springs surround Beth Shean. The foundations of a series of Canaanite temples and palaces have been discovered.

The New Testament city that grew up around the tel was called Scythopolis. The excavated remains of this lower city include a theatre, hippodrome, baths, Graeco-Roman temples, and an amphitheater. The public buildings covered a vast area here in New Testament times. The private houses are probably buried beneath the modern city of Beth Shean.

THE HISTORY OF BETH SHEAN AND SCYTOPOLIS

The name Beth Shean means "house of security" or "tranquility". Founded as early as the fifth millennium B.C., Beth Shean was already an important Canaanite city when first mentioned in Egyptian texts about 2,000 B.C. This writing, called an execration text, cursed the city for its independence from Egypt.

The Egyptians eventually took control of the city and it became an Egyptian military fort until the

QUICK FACTS

Beth Shean is located at the intersection of the Jordan and Jezreel Valleys. The city was located near a main Egyptian road and a ford on the Jordan River.

Though allotted to Manasseh, it remained unconquered until David's reign.

Saul and Jonathan were killed nearby, and Saul's armor hung in the temple of the Philistines.

REFERENCES

Joshua 17:11, 16

Judges 1:27

Samuel 31:8-12

2 Samuel 21:12

1 Kings 4:12

1 Chronicles 7:29

end of the 11th century B.C. The presence of Philistine clay coffins with human features on them indicates the Philistines were stationed there as mercenary troops under the Egyptians.

The Israelites conquered Beth Shean during the reign of David, and it later became part of Solomon's fifth administrative district. However, Israelite control was rather short-lived. Pharaoh Shishak reconquered the city soon after Solomon's death.

About 700 years later, the city was resettled as a Greek colony and named Scythopolis, meaning "City of the Scythians". Jewish control was briefly restored under the Maccabees, who expelled all Gentiles from the city. It became a Gentile city again when the Romans took over. The city prospered and became the largest city of the Decapolis or the Ten Cities (Matthew 4:25), with a population that included Gentiles, Samaritans, and Jews.

By the sixth century A.D., the city was mostly Christian. In the seventh century, it was conquered by Muslims, and subsequently destroyed by an earthquake. The city never recovered.

THE ARCHAEOLOGY OF BETH SHEAN AND SCYTOPOLIS

Beth Shean consists of an upper city on the tel and a lower city to the south and west of the tel. The site has been excavated intermittently since 1921, revealing the remains of over 20 layers of occupation.

Among the most interesting remains on the tel are a series of temples, built one on top of the other over a period of 500 years. A 15th century BC temple includes an inscription to a god, "Mekal, the Baal (lord) of Beth Shean."

During the time of Pharaoh Ramses II of Egypt, there were two temples, which were continually used until about 1,000 B.C. These are perhaps the temples in which the Philistines put Saul's armor as a trophy (1 Samuel 31:10). Other important finds include two large standing stones with inscriptions boasting of the military successes of Pharaoh Seti I against the "Apiru" which could mean the Hebrews, in about 1,300 B.C.

The most spectacular remains in the lower city are the Roman public buildings and streets.

The Roman theater is the best-preserved example in Israel. It once held over 7,000 people. A street named Palladius, after a governor of the province, runs from the tel to the theater. This street began with a large gateway that towered more than 40 feet. The street was lined with marble columns on each side. The columns supported roofs for a covered sidewalk.

Along this street, a semicircular building featured a large mosaic depicting Tyche, the good luck guardian of the city, holding a cornucopia. The bath complex west of Palladius Street consisted of more than the usual three pools. There were nine large halls, all with marble mosaic floors. Two additional pools were located at the ends of covered porches.

A Roman temple stood on a nearby corner. A statue of Marcus Aurelius (161-180 A.D.), the "philosopher emperor," was found in front of the temple. About 900 feet from the theater was the amphitheater. This oval structure, built in the second century A.D. was the arena for gladiator sports. It once held about 6,000 people.

A synagogue built around the fourth or fifth century A.D. was found west of the city. To the north, a Samaritan synagogue was excavated, with a mosaic floor depicting the Ark of the Law.

BETH SHEAN AND SCYTOPOLIS IN THE BIBLE

Beth Shean and its surrounding towns were located in territory allotted to the Israelite tribe of Manasseh. Like other heavily fortified Canaanite cities, the Israelites were unable to conquer the city for several centuries.

The city was under the control of the Philistines when Saul was killed in the battle on Mount Gilboa, just south of Beth Shean. After the battle, the bodies of Saul and his three sons Jonathan, Abinadab, and Malki-Shua were taken by the Philistines and hung on the walls of Beth Shean (1 Samuel 31:10). Saul's armor was placed in the temple in Beth Shean (1 Chronicles 10:10; 1 Samuel 31:10). The Israelites of Jabesh Gilead came by night and took down their bodies, giving them a proper burial.

Eventually, the Israelites won the upper hand and conquered Beth Shean. The Bible does not mention this conquest, but it probably occurred during the reign of David. The city became part of Solomon's fifth administrative district (1 Kings 4:12) before being conquered by Pharaoh Shishak (1 Kings 14:25).

The Bible does not mention the city again. In the New Testament, people came to Jesus from the Decapolis, the ten Greek cities that included Beth Shean, but there is no specific mention of this city.

WHAT CAN WE LEARN FROM BETH SHEAN AND SCYTOPOLIS?

Saul's downfall can be traced to his earlier encounter with the Amalekites. In 1 Samuel 15, God, through the prophet Samuel, instructed Saul to destroy the Amelekite nation. Saul, however, disobeyed the instructions by sparing King Agag and the best of the livestock. Saul's excuses for disobedience fell on deaf ears as Samuel gave God's verdict upon the act:

> And Samuel said,
> "Has the Lord as great delight in burnt offerings and sacrifices,
> as in obeying the voice of the Lord?
>
> Behold, to obey is better than sacrifice,
> and to listen than the fat of rams.
>
> For rebellion is as the sin of divination,
> and presumption is as iniquity and idolatry.
>
> Because you have rejected the word of the Lord,
> he has also rejected you from being king."
>
> 1 SAMUEL 15:22-23

Saul considered incomplete obedience to be "close enough" to be acceptable to the Lord. God viewed it as a complete rejection of His authority. When we become arbiters of good and evil, we set ourselves in the place of God. In this case, Saul's actions cost him the kingdom. The mighty had fallen.

We face this same disobedience today when we leave part of our heats unconquered by God's love and forgiveness. Our conduct sometimes reflects those areas of our lives left unconquered. We must make a decision to eliminate these areas, replacing them with the reflection of Christ's love.

> "Let all bitterness and wrath and anger and clamor and slander be
> put away from you, along with all malice. Be kind to one another,
> tenderhearted, forgiving one another, as God in Christ forgave you."
>
> EPHESIANS 4:31-32

SHECHEM

A PLACE TO REMEMBER GOD'S PROMISES

"Abram passed through the land to the place at Shechem, to the oak of Moreh. At that time the Canaanites were in the land. Then the Lord appeared to Abram and said, "To your offspring I will give this land." So he built there an altar to the Lord, who had appeared to him."

BACKGROUND, ARCHAEOLOGY, AND SIGNIFICANCE:

SHECHEM IN HISTORY

Shechem was a place of religious significance for many nations besides the Israelites, including the Canaanites, Samaritans, and much later, the Romans. One author describes Shechem as a "city of altars, sacred pillars and trees, temples, covenants, covenant renewal, and political confirmation ceremonies."[7] Like most biblical cities, Shechem began as a small village sometime around 4,000 B.C. It was not until about 2,000 years later the inhabitants fortified the city and built what appears to be a "sacred area" for religious rituals.[8]

Like its northern neighbor Megiddo, Shechem was frequently subject to the warring tides of rival nations, first taken by Sesostris III of Egypt in the second millennium B.C.[9] The Amarna letters, historic Egyptian records, mention the land-grabbing efforts of King Lab'ayu of Shechem in contradiction to his previous pledge of loyalty to Egypt.[10] The city was leveled in 1550 B.C. and rebuilt sometime before the time of the Judges.

Judges 9 records the conspiracy of Abimelech to take over the kingship of Israel. In the process he violently overthrew Shechem (cf. Judg. 9:42-49), which may align with evidence of Shechem's destruction during the 12th century B.C. The city appears to have remained in disrepair until after the reign of Solomon. The city was refortified and made an administrative center of Israel until its destruction by the Assyrians after the fall of the Northern Kingdom in 722 B.C. Shechem was largely uninhabited until the middle of the

QUICK FACTS

The ancient city of Shechem is now called Tell Balatah and sits about thirty miles north of Jerusalem towards the east end of the pass between Mount Ebal and Mount Gerizim.

Shechem's location at the crux of two vital trade routes gave its rulers oversight of the 'highway' that cut through the pass connecting to Megiddo in the north and Jerusalem and Hebron to the south.

Given the city's precariously exposed perch on the lower slope of Mount Ebal, defending Shechem required significant fortification projects. Incidentally, "Shechem" is the Hebrew word for "shoulder".

----

7 DeVries, *Cities of the Biblical World.*
8 Ibid., 235.
9 Ibid.
10 Ibid.

REFERENCES

Genesis 12:6-7

Genesis 33:18-20

Joshua 8:30-35
(implied in v. 33)

Joshua 20:7; 21:20-21; 24:1

Judges 9:1-2, 42-49

1 Kings 12:1, 25

fourth century B.C. after which point it flourished as the religious center of the Samaritans.

Shechem's peace ended in 107 B.C. when John Hycranus destroyed the city. Although Shechem was never rebuilt, emperor Vespasian chose the site for the city he called Neapolis, which literally means "new city". A temple to Zeus later adorned the brow of Mount Gerizim where the Samaritan temple once stood.

THE ARCHAEOLOGY OF SHECHEM

The excavation of Shechem, conducted primarily in two stints, 1913-1934 and 1956-1973, revealed the city's first "substantial defense system,"[11] built sometime around 1800 B.C. The defense system included a large "embankment" that buttressed by a "mud-brick wall."[12] This wall was later rebuilt with stone.

Excavations of this same period also unearthed the original "temple complex" with its network of rooms bordering a "central courtyard" which held the "sacred pillars."[13] The temple was later elevated and enlarged, which also increased the city's fortifications perhaps giving it the designation "temple fortress."[14]

Archaeologists did not find a "destruction layer"[15] that could be dated to the time of the Israelite conquest of Canaan, a fact which squares with the omission of Shechem from the biblical record of conquered cities.[16] There is, however, evidence of the city's destruction in the 12th century B.C., which again likely coincides with the biblical account of Abimelech's rage against

....

11 DeVries, *Cities of the Biblical World.*, 235.

12 Ibid.

13 Ibid.

14 Ibid.

15 Ibid., 236.

16 Ibid.

Shechem in Judges 9.[17] Further evidence was found of the city's rebuilding in the time between Rehoboam and the Assyrian exile, at which point the site yields signs of yet another demolition, this time by the Assyrians.[18] Archaeologists can also identify signs of the city's renaissance at the hands of the Samaritans, including homes, new city walls, and the temple on Mount Gerizim.

SHECHEM IN THE BIBLE

Beginning with Abraham, the city of Shechem was a place at which God's people commemorated covenant commitment. After Abram sets out from Haran for Canaan in obedience to God's command in Genesis 12:1-3, the Lord again appears to Abram once he reaches Canaan to reiterate His covenant promise in Genesis 12:6-7. It is here in Shechem that Abram builds an altar to mark the place in which he again received God's promise. Later, Jacob also built an altar in Shechem after meeting Esau, presumably in gratitude to God for answering his request for safety (cf. Gen. 32:12).

During the Israelite conquest of Canaan, after Achan and his family are destroyed for their greed and the city of Ai finally falls to the Israelites (cf. Josh. 7:10-8:29), Joshua led the people of Israel to Shechem to renew their covenant with the Lord. Near Shechem on Mount Ebal, opposite of Mount Gerizim, Joshua built an altar to the Lord, offering sacrifices and reading aloud the law given to Moses (cf. Josh. 8:30-35).

This appears to be the periodic covenant renewal ceremony prescribed by Moses in Deuteronomy 27-28 and 31:9-13.[19] In fact, Moses specifies that when the Israelites enter Canaan they are to set up an altar on Mount Ebal, as Joshua does in Joshua 8, and from there six of the twelve tribes were to proclaim the curses for disobedience to the Lord's covenant. Conversely, the other six tribes were to stand on Mount Gerizim and proclaim the promised blessings for obeying the Lord's commands.[20] Michael Harbin suggests that these guidelines were not merely ritualistic details, but rather the provision of a "dramatic visual image."[21] This is because Mount Ebal, the peak from which the curses were to be proclaimed, was brown and "barren" in stark contrast to the green forests

17 Ibid.

18 Ibid.

19 Michael Harbin, *The Promise and the Blessing: A Historical Survey of the Old and New Testaments* (Grand Rapids, MI: Zondervan, 2005).

20 Ibid.

21 Ibid. 172

that adorned Mount Gerizim.[22] The contrast between the lifelessness of Ebal and the lush woods of Gerizim was meant to represent the choice between "life and death, blessing and curse," (Deut. 30:19) laid before the Israelites in the covenantal law. At the end of his life, Joshua will deliver his "farewell address"[23] and lead the Israelites in renewing the covenant again at Shechem (cf. Josh. 24).

From this time on, Shechem was "one of the major religious and political centers in ancient Israel."[24] During the time of the Judges the upstart Abimelech would be the first to grab for the throne of Israel by making his claim at Shechem (cf. Judg. 9). After the death of Solomon, Solomon's son Rehoboam chose to have a coronation at Shechem, presumably in addition to the customary anointing in Jerusalem. As the Scholar DeVries notes, Rehoboam's decision to journey to Shechem for a second anointing underscores the importance of the city as a "political center in the north."[25] As 1 Kings relates, however, Rehoboam's journey to Shechem was not enough to secure the city's support and, when he refused to concede to the people's desires (cf. 1 Kgs. 12:1-15), the tribes in the north made Jeroboam their king and established their capital in Shechem.

WHAT CAN WE LEARN FROM SHECHEM?

Behold, how good and pleasant it is when brothers dwell in unity!

It is like the precious oil on the head, running down on the beard,

on the beard of Aaron, running down on the collar of his robes!

It is like the dew of Hermon, which falls on the mountains of Zion!

For there the Lord has commanded the blessing, life forevermore.

PSALM 133

By all accounts, ancient Shechem was a modest village, a community of fisherman and hunters, Jews and Gentiles alike. Hailing from Shechem would not have afforded fisherman like Peter, Andrew, and Phillip any clout or great opportunities, and, in fact, they were considered "uneducated, common men" (said specifically of Peter and John, Acts 4:13). And yet, these simple fishermen followed Jesus' call to follow Him, which made all the difference for their life and ministry.

....

22 Ibid.

23 DeVries, *Cities of the Biblical World*, 233.

24 Ibid., 231.

25 Ibid., 234.

The calling of Peter, Andrew, and John, these uneducated Shechem boys, reminds us, in the words of Paul, that God often uses:

> *"But God chose what is foolish in the world to shame the wise; God chose what is weak in the world to shame the strong; God chose what is low and despised in the world, even things that are not, to bring to nothing things that are, so that no human being might boast in the presence of God."*
>
> 1 CORINTHIANS 1:27-29

We can therefore rejoice that no matter our background, our education, our pedigree, or any man-made pedigree, God chooses and equips us through the Holy Spirit to do good works prepared beforehand (Eph. 2:10).

> *"Therefore, if anyone is in Christ, he is a new creation. The old has passed away; behold, the new has come."*
>
> 2 CORINTHINANS 5:17

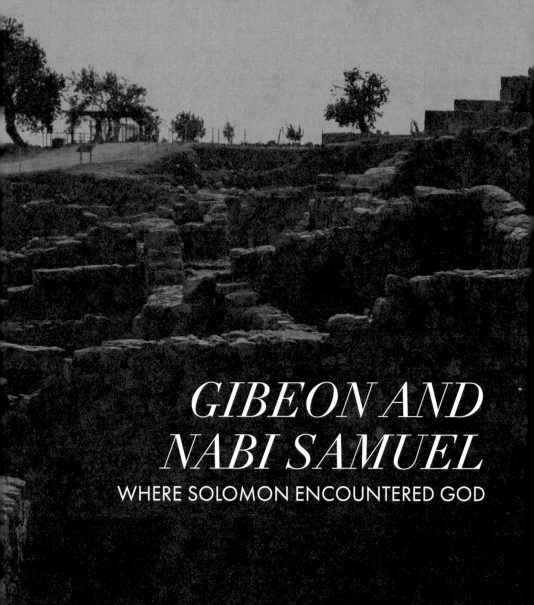

GIBEON AND NABI SAMUEL

WHERE SOLOMON ENCOUNTERED GOD

"At Gibeon the Lord appeared to Solomon in a dream by
night, and God said, "Ask what I shall give you."

1 KINGS 3:5

BACKGROUND, ARCHAEOLOGY, AND SIGNIFICANCE

THE HISTORY OF GIBEON AND NABI SAMUEL

Based on archaeological evidence, Gibeon is believed to have been settled in sometime at the beginning of the second millennium B.C[26]. The population of Gibeon seemed to dwindle later in the second millennium[27]. The golden age of the city came in the seventh century B.C. when Gibeon was known for its prominent role in the creation and distribution of wine.

THE ARCHAEOLOGY OF GIBEON AND NABI SAMUEL

The site of ancient Gibeon, modern-day el-Jib, was substantiated with the "discovery of 31 jar handles inscribed with the name Gibeon,"[28] likely related to the city's role in wine production. Archeological work at the site of ancient Gibeon revealed "a sophisticated water system including a huge circular pool hewn out of stone."[29] This finding corresponds with the references to the "great pool" at Gibeon in the Old Testament (cf. 2 Sam. 2:13; Jer. 41:12).[30] Excavations also revealed tombs from the second millennium and what was likely the city's first defensive wall built sometime in the 12th century.[31]

GIBEON AND NABI SAMUEL IN THE BIBLE

Gibeon is first mentioned in Joshua 9 as the native country of a group of Canaanite deceivers who travel to Joshua and the Israelites. Joshua

....
26 Myers, et. al. Eerdmans *Dictionary of the Bible.*
27 Ibid.
28 Ibid., 502.
29 Ibid.
30 Ibid.
31 Ibid.

QUICK FACTS

Gibeon is a seven-mile journey from Jerusalem and located at a central juncture in the hill country of Israel.

The city is positioned on the outskirts of a large flat region in central Benjamin, a natural battleground between Israel and Judah.

The Tent of Meeting was erected at Gibeon and Nabi Samuel before the construction of the Temple in Jerusalem.

REFERENCES

Joshua 9:3ff

1 Samuel 10:5

2 Samuel 2:12-17; 20:8; 21:1-14

1 Kings 3:2-5

1 Chronicles 16:39; 21:29

2 Chronicles 1:3

Jeremiah 28:1; 41:11-18

Nehemiah 3:7-8

and the Israelites did not ask the Lord where these travelers came from, and the Israelites were tricked into signing a treaty explicitly against God's command (cf. Ex. 23:32-33). From the time of the conquest of the land, but particularly during the reigns of David and Solomon, Gibeon was one of the Israelites' "high places" (1 Kings 3:2) where people offered sacrifices in the absence of a central place for corporate worship.[32] It was here that Solomon inquired of the Lord and where the Lord famously appeared to Solomon, offering to fulfill his most earnest request (cf. 1 Kings 3:5ff). After the death of Solomon, Gibeon became a place of violence and bloodshed in the war between Israel and Judah.

WHAT CAN WE LEARN FROM GIBEON AND NABI SAMUEL?

Throughout the Old Testament, "high places" most commonly refers to cultic sites for the worship of pagan gods. The Temple at Jerusalem was built to house the ark of the covenant, on which the very presence of God was pleased to dwell, and represented the singular authority and unity of Yahweh God. Unlike the deities of the Canaanite religions, God does not share power with a pantheon of other gods nor can He be approached without a suitable mediator. In Old Testament times, the High Priest was the mediator between God and His people. Hebrews 10 explains how the risen Christ now fulfills this role for believers. It was vital that the Israelites recognize the Temple as the one true place of worship to the one true God.[33]

The existence of the high places in Israel, including the one at Gibeon, served as a temporary place for the Tent of Meeting. This demonstrates God's patience with His people as they learned what it meant to follow Him. While Solomon arranged for the building of the Temple, the Lord was pleased to meet with him (cf. 2 Chron. 1:3, 7-13). In the same type of way, God is patient with us in the process of our sanctification. He Himself orchestrates the process by which we can become more like Christ, and He understands us and shows fatherly compassion toward us:

....

32 Randall Price, and H. Wayne House, Zondervan Handbook of Biblical Archaeology (Grand Rapids, MI: HarperCollins, 2017).

33 1 Kings 11:1-8 and 1 Kings 12:25-33 tell the sad story of what happened in Israel as a result of Solomon and Jeroboam building other places of worship, even those supposedly intended for Yahweh.

"For He knows our frame; He remembers that we are dust. As for man, his days are like grass; he flourishes like a flower of the field; for the wind passes over it, and it is gone, and its place knows it no more. But the steadfast love of the LORD is from everlasting to everlasting on those who fear Him, and His righteousness to children's children, to those who keep his covenant and remember to do his commandments."

PSALM 103:14-18

HERODIUM

WHERE GOD DELIVERED HIS PEOPLE

"At Gibeon the Lord appeared to Solomon in a dream by
night,and God said, "Ask what I shall give you.""

1 KINGS 3:5

BACKGROUND, ARCHAEOLOGY, AND SIGNIFICANCE

THE GEOGRAPHY OF HERODIUM

Standing 758 meters above sea level, the highest peak in the Judean Desert, with views overlooking the desert, the mountains of Moab, and the Judean Hills; stands the truncated cone-shaped hill where King Herod built his palace fortress at Herodium.

THE HISTORY OF HERODIUM

Herod the Great lived in luxury and spared no expense on his many palaces.

THE ARCHAEOLOGY OF HERODIUM

Excavations of the palace at Herodium unearthed the remains of Herod's personal rooms, a garden/courtyard, a "dining hall," and a "full Roman bath with hot, cold, and warm rooms."[37] The water for the bath was channeled four miles via aqueduct from the city Artas[38] to fill a total of five cisterns, four installed below ground and one above ground.[39]

The palace was fortified by "two concentric circular walls," the outermost wall encompassing an area of approximately 31,000 square feet and partitioned from the inner by an almost twelve-foot wide "corridor."[40] To make it more difficult for assailants to breach the fortress, Herod had the outer wall surrounded by a mound of "dirt

QUICK FACTS

The hill that marks Herodium is the site of Herod's "desert palace/fortress"[34] approximately seven miles outside Jerusalem and three miles to the southeast of Bethlehem.[35]

Herodium was the third-largest fortress in the entire Roman Empire.[36]

REFERENCES

There are no references to Herodium by name in the Bible.

34 Alfred Hoerth and John McRay, *Bible Archaeology: An Exploration of the History and Culture of Early Civilizations* (Grand Rapids, MI: Baker Books, 2005), 200.

35 John McRay, *Archaeology and the New Testament* (Grand Rapids, MI: Baker Book House, 1991).

36 Hoerth and McRay, *Bible Archaeology.*

37 Hoerth and McRay, *Bible Archaeology*, 201.

38 McRay, *Archaeology and the NT*, 129.

39 Hoerth and McRay, *Bible Archaeology.*

and gravel,"[41] giving the fortress the appearance of a beehive or "cone-shaped volcano."[42]

On lower ground at the base of Herodium's hill Herod commissioned a "lower palace covering 45 acres,"[43] in which he installed another set of personal rooms, and a "magnificent garden containing a huge colonnaded pool with a circular island in the middle."[44] Near the lower palace Herod also built buildings for administrative purposes. Excavations of these buildings reveal a separate bath for servants the other attendants.[45] Based on Josephus' records, Herod is believed to be buried somewhere near the pool outside his lower palace, although the location of his tomb is still unknown.[46]

HERODIUM IN THE BIBLE

There are no explicit references to Herodium in the Bible.

WHAT CAN WE LEARN FROM HERODIUM?

Herod the Great was a capricious and greedy ruler. Although Jewish by heritage, he enjoyed his glut of the Roman riches as a benefit of his position as governor of Judea. Herod sought to make his mark throughout the region by conducting ostentatious building campaigns, palaces, fortresses, including Herodium, and even the building of the Second Temple in Jerusalem, all primarily as monuments to himself.

Like many people blinded by power and greed, Herod expected his legacy to be enduring and illustrious. Today, his mighty fortresses and lavish castles are mere skeletons of their former glory. Herodium is a warning against the deceptiveness of power and riches, a call to lay hold of "the life that is truly life" (1 Tim. 6:19). Herodium is a reminder that although it may seem as though evildoers prosper and enjoy the wealth of the world, in the end God has the final word.

....

41 Ibid.
42 McRay, Archaeology and the NT, 129.
43 Hoerth and McRay, Bible Archaeology.
44 Ibid.
45 Ibid.
46 Ibid.

Fret not yourself because of evildoers; be not envious of wrongdoers!
Commit your way to the LORD; trust in Him, and He will act.
He will bring forth your righteousness as the light,
and your justice as the noonday.

PSALM 37:1, 5-6

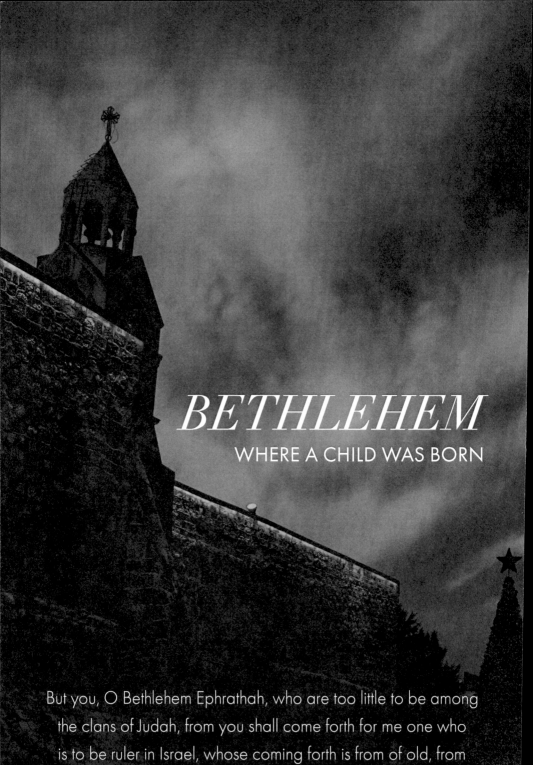

BETHLEHEM
WHERE A CHILD WAS BORN

But you, O Bethlehem Ephrathah, who are too little to be among the clans of Judah, from you shall come forth for me one who is to be ruler in Israel, whose coming forth is from of old, from

BACKGROUND, ARCHAEOLOGY, AND SIGNIFICANCE

THE HISTORY OF BETHLEHEM

Although the details of Bethlehem's founding and initial development are not known, record of the city has been identified as early as "the fourteenth century B.C.E."[48] in the Amarna Tablets. These tablets are among the records of Ab-di-heba, Jerusalem's governor at that time, and indicate that at some point in that time period "Bit Lahmi . . . has fallen into the hands of the marauding 'Apiru people."[49] The city seems to have also been called by the name Ephrathah (cf. Gen. 35:19; 48:7)

THE ARCHAEOLOGY OF BETHLEHEM

According to Justin Martyr, as early as the second century A.D. Christians "revered a certain limestone cave as the site of the birth of the Messiah."[50] However, many sites sacred to Christians and Jews were laid waste when the Jews were driven out of Bethlehem and Jerusalem later in the second century A.D.[51]

The recognized site of Jesus' birth in Bethlehem likely remained in disrepair until the original Church of the Nativity was built with the patronage of Constantine's mother, Helena, the dedication of which took place on May 31, 339.[52] Additionally, Jerome is believed to have written the Vulgate in a cave close to the Church of the Nativity.[53]

....
47 Myers, et. al., *Eerdmans Dictionary of the Bible*, 172
48 Myers, et. al., *Eerdmans Dictionary of the Bible*.
49 Ibid., 173.
50 Ibid.
51 Ibid.
52 Ibid.
53 Ibid.

QUICK FACTS

Bethlehem is situated east of the Hebron road on the edge of the "Judean hill country," about five miles southwest of Jerusalem.[47]

In Hebrew, Bethlehem means "house of bread," and is the birthplace of Jesus, as promised in Micah 5:2.

REFERENCES

Genesis 35:19; 48:7

Joshua 19:15-16

Judges 12:8-10; 17:7; 19:1

Ruth 1:1, 19

1 Samuel 16:1, 4

2 Samuel 23:13-17

1 Chronicles 2:51

2 Chronicles 11:5-6

Micah 5:2

Matthew 2:1-8, 16

Luke 2:4, 15

In 1 Chronicles 2:51 Caleb's grandson Salma is designated as the "father of Bethlehem,"[54] and Israelites are believed to have lived there first during the rule of the Judges.[55] Bethlehem was the hometown of the Levite who abused his priestly office by stewarding and directing the worship of a cast idol in Micah's household (cf. Judges 17:7).[56] Bethlehem was also the hometown of the unnamed concubine whose brutal murder incited "civil war against the tribe of Benjamin" after her master distributed pieces of her corpse throughout Israel.[57]

However, Bethlehem also has great significance in redemption history, first as the home of Elimelech and Naomi. It was Naomi who returned to Bethlehem with her Moabite daughter-in-law Ruth following the death of her husband and sons. It was here in Bethlehem where Ruth met and married the righteous kinsman-redeemer Boaz and gave birth to Obed, the grandfather of King David.[58]

Not surprisingly, Bethlehem grew in popularity and influence following the rise of King David to the throne of Israel (1 Sam. 16:1-13). During the reign of Saul, the city housed a "military outpost"[59] for the Philistines (cf. 2 Sam. 23:13-17), who were later driven out by Rehoboam, becoming part of a 14-city "defensive network around Jerusalem"[60] (cf. 2 Chron. 11:5-12). In Ezra 2:21, 123 men from Bethlehem are recorded in the company of those returning to Israel from exile in Babylon.[61]

Obviously, all of history hinges on Bethlehem as the birthplace of Jesus early in the first century A.D. as foretold in Micah 5:2. As Matthew's Gospel indicates, the Jewish authorities in Jerusalem knew Micah's prophecy when the Magi arrived seeking the newborn King. After confirming the Magi's interpretation of the auspicious sign in the sky, Herod commanded that all male children in Bethlehem under the age of two be killed.[62]

....

54 Ibid.
55 Ibid.
56 Ibid.
57 Ibid.
58 Ibid. 173.
59 Ibid.
60 Ibid.
61 Ibid.
62 Ibid.

WHAT CAN WE LEARN FROM BETHLEHEM?

Although references to Bethlehem are scattered throughout the Old Testament, out of the 39 Old Testament books, only one mentions Bethlehem's particularly significant role in redemption history as the birthplace of God's chosen ruler, the Messiah.

Micah 5:2 states that even though Bethlehem was "too little to be among the clans of Judah," God would still bring forth from Bethlehem "one who is to be ruler in Israel, whose coming forth is form of old, from ancient days." This chosen ruler would not be born in Jerusalem, the city of the Temple and religious festivals. Instead, he would be born in Bethlehem, the place of David's anointing. This was a sign God would fulfill the promise He made to David in 2 Samuel 7:16.

Hundreds of years passed from the time of Micah's prophecy to the birth of Christ. The prophecy itself may have even faded into distant memory. Micah's words rang clear when the Magi arrived in Jerusalem. The leaders knew God did not abandon His plan or His promise to His people. This gives us hope in those seasons of waiting.

It's in the 'in-between' times when it may feel like God has abandoned you. It's easy for God's promises to fade in our memory. This is when the story of Bethlehem, the city of promise for the Messiah's birth, reminds us again of God's supernatural plan. God doesn't forget us. He chooses the right time and the right place to fulfill His promises to us. We only need to wait on Him to move when He's ready.

> *"And the angel said to them, "Fear not, for behold, I bring you good news of great joy that will be for all the people. For unto you is born this day in the city of David a Savior, who is Christ the Lord."*

LUKE 2:10-11

BET SHEMESH

WHERE THE ARK RETURNED

Now the people of Beth-shemesh were reaping their wheat
harvest in the valley. And when they lifted up their eyes and saw
the ark, they rejoiced to see it.

BACKGROUND, ARCHAEOLOGY, AND SIGNIFICANCE

THE GEOGRAPHY OF BET SHEMESH

The Shephelah region, home to Bet Shemesh, often functioned in the past as a natural divider between the people of the hills and their often-stronger enemies who lived along the coastal plain. Unfortunately, this means that many terrible battles have taken place near Bet Shemesh.

THE HISTORY OF BET SHEMESH

At the time of ancient Israel, Bet Shemesh was a city in the Shephelah ("western foothills") region, a geopolitically thin band of land that divided the land of the Philistines from the hills of Judah. Archaeologists working at Bet Shemesh have identified six layers of remains, each corresponding to a period in the city's life from the Early Bronze Age to the Persian period and Hellenistic period.[65]

Sometime in the Middle Bronze Age is the likely time period when the city's first fortification was built: a wall surrounding the city with two towers.[66] A similar fortification with additional towers was added in later years, a detail that stands out due to Egyptian policy in the region forbidding its vassal cities from building defenses.[67] This leaves open the possibility that Beth-Shemesh was actually an "independent city-state" at the time of the additions.[68]

63   Allen C. Myers, Astrid B. Beck, and David Noel Freedman, eds., Eerdmans Dictionary of the Bible (Grand Rapids, MI: W.B. Eerdmans, 2000), 175, http://www.questiaschool.com/read/118845606/eerdmans-dictionary-of-the-bible.

64   Ibid., 176.

65   Ibid.

66   Ibid.

67   Ibid.

68   Ibid.

THE ARCHAEOLOGY OF BET SHEMESH

Archaeologists have discovered remains of houses, many with "court-yards paved with white plaster," containers presumably used for storage, "a furnace for smelting ore" as well as several silos and cisterns for storage of food and water.[69] Additionally, a tablet inscribed with Ugaritic cuneiform script as well as a potsherd with the Canaanite alphabet were also found.[70] Excavations of later strata reveal a change in defensive fortifications and more residential dwellings.[71] The ancient city was ultimately destroyed during the Babylon invasion of Judah in 586 BC, as revealed by a "destruction layer" in the city's strata.[72]

BET SHEMESH IN THE BIBLE

Bet Shemesh is first mentioned in the Bible as a part of Naphatali's tribal inheritance in the land of Canaan (cf. Judg. 1:33).[73] However, like many other frontier cities in the land of Canaan, the Israelites did not fully take possession of the city as commanded by God but they conscripted many of its existing inhabitants into forced labor.

1 Samuel 4-6 tells of Israel's defeat by the Philistines and the subsequent capture of the Ark of the Covenant, which the Israelites brought into battle as a kind of good luck charm (cf. 1 Sam. 4:3). The Lord afflicted the Philistines with "tumors" and sent a plague of mice to "ravage" their land (1 Sam. 6:4). The Philistines returned the ark to Israel with a "guilt offering" (1 Sam. 6:4) by placing the ark on a cart and releasing the cart onto the road, saying:

> *"If it goes up on the way to its own land, to Beth-shemesh, then it is*
> *He [YHWH] who has done us this great harm, but if not, then we*
> *shall know that it is not His hand that struck us; it happened to us*
> *by coincidence."*

1 SAMUEL 6:9

When the cow-driven cart did indeed head toward Beth-shemesh, it was a testament of the Lord's power and might to the Philistines. When the driverless cart arrived in Beth-shemesh, it was spotted by the people of Beth-shemesh reaping their wheat harvest, there was a great celebra-

---

69 Ibid. 176.

70 Ibid.

71 Ibid.

72 Ibid. and Currid and Barrett, ESV Bible Atlas, 174.

73 Ibid.

130

tion and worship to the Lord. Ultimately, however, the people of Beth-shemesh also experienced the Lord's righteous power when "he struck some of the men of Beth-shemesh, because they looked upon the ark of the LORD" (1 Sam. 6:19). After this, the people of Beth-shemesh sent to the people of Kiriath-jearim to take the art.

During the days of the divided kingdom, Bet-Sehmesh was also the site of a conflict between Amaziah, king of Judah and Jehoash, king of Israel. After instigating a needless fight with Jehoash, Amaziah met Jehoash in battle at Bet-Shemesh in which the army of Judah was soundly routed and Amaziah himself captured. This led to the destruction of Jerusalem's wall and plunder of the temple (cf. 1 Kngs.14:8-14).

During the reign of Ahaz, the Philistines raided Judah's territory and captured many cities, including Bet-Shemesh (cf. 2 Chron. 28:18).[74] The context of 2 Chronicles 28 describes the Philistine raids as well as the conquering of Judah by Tiglath-Pileser of Assyria to be part of the Lord's punishment for Ahaz's unfaithfulness and pride (cf. 2 Chron. 28:19-21).

WHAT CAN WE LEARN FROM BET SHEMESH?

The story of Beth-shemesh recorded in 1 Samuel 6 is both a beautiful picture of God's commitment to His people and a sobering reminder of His holiness. The LORD showed His desire to be with His people, despite their flippant wielding of the ark as a good luck charm, by sending a clear message to the Philistines, demonstrating His "superiority over Dagon" [a Philistine god].[75] Sadly, the LORD did not spare those of His own people who did not treat His Presence among them with the due respect. This aspect of the story is admittedly mysterious and may be best to remain a mystery to us. The people's question in 1 Samuel 6:20, "Who is able to stand before the LORD, this holy God?" is allowed to hang in the air.

And yet, readers of the Old Testament today can rejoice because God has made a way for us to stand before Him through Christ. It's challenging for us as for modern-day believers to cultivate both proper reverence for God's holiness and complete confidence in His love and commitment to us in Christ.

The story of the ark at Beth-shemesh reminds us that we worship an unquestionably holy, deeply loving, and supremely powerful God

....

74 Ibid.

75 Antony F. Campbell, 1 Samuel (Grand Rapids, MI: Eerdmans, 2003), 75, http://www.questiaschool.com/read/119906313/1-samuel.

who even in His intimacy with us through Christ will nevertheless remain mysterious.

> *"Then the men of Beth-shemesh said, "Who is able to stand before the LORD, this holy God? And to whom shall he go up away from us?"*

1 SAMUEL 6:20

THE VALLEY OF ELAH

DAVID VS. GOLIATH

Then David said to the Philistine, "You come to me with a sword and with a spear and with la javelin, but I come to you in the name of the LORD of hosts, the God of the armies of Israel, whom you have defied."

BACKGROUND, ARCHAEOLOGY, AND SIGNIFICANCE

Like Bet Shemesh, the Valley of Elah was part of the Shephelah region and therefore, a likely battleground between the peoples of the plains, such as the Philistines in 1 Samuel 17, and the people of the hill country, the Israelites. The oft-told story of David and Goliath takes historical shape in the Valley of Elah.

1 Samuel 17:3 says the rival nations of Israel and Philistia stood on opposite mountain faces on either side of the Valley of Elah, Philistia on the west and Israel on the east, awaiting the ensuing conflict. The valley formed a sort of natural battle line and marks the place in which David and Goliath met in combat, with their respective comrades looking on from higher ground.

WHAT CAN WE LEARN FROM THE VALLEY OF ELAH?

Visiting this fabled battlefront is a poignant reminder of the LORD's supremacy and might. Although many childhood renditions of the story focus on David's bravery, it is important to remember the LORD is the uncontested Victor in the confrontation with Goliath. In 1 Samuel 17:26 David identifies Goliath as one who "defies the arms of the living God," (emphasis added), and in 1 Samuel 17:37 David responds to Saul's doubts about his ability as an untrained youth to face a mighty warrior by drawing on God's previous faithfulness to him: "The LORD who delivered me form the paw of the lion and the paw of the bear will deliver me from the hand of this Philistine"

And again, David displayed his unwavering confidence in God to win the battle in 1 Samuel 17:45: "You [Goliath] come to me with a sword and with a spear and with a javelin, *but I come*

QUICK FACTS

The Valley of Elah is located approximately eight or nine miles southwest of Bethlehem and served as a segue into the Judean hill country.

This valley is where the famous standoff between Israel and Philistia occurred in which the young David slew the Philistine giant Goliath.

REFERENCES

1 Samuel 17:2-3, 19

to you in the name of the LORD of hosts, the God of the armies of Israel."
(emphasis added)

In 1 Samuel 17:46-47 David declared to Goliath that God will give David
the victory for God's glory: "that all the earth may know there is a God
in Israel, that all this assembly may know that the LORD saves not with
sword and spear. For the battle is the LORD's" (1 Samuel 17:46c-47a).

In the midst of our own battles with the enemies of Satan, our sinful desires, and the influences of the world, we can lose sight of God's power to
work for His glory and our good in and through our struggle.

"He leads me in paths of righteousness for his name's sake."

PSALM 23:3

MARESHAH & MORESHETH GAT

WHERE GOD DELIVERED HIS PEOPLE

Zerah the Ethiopian came out against them with an army of a million men and 300 chariots, and came as far as Mareshah. 10 And Asa went out to meet him, and they drew up their lines of battle in the Valley of Zephathah at Mareshah.

2 CHRONICLES 14:9-10

BACKGROUND, ARCHAEOLOGY, AND SIGNIFICANCE

THE GEOGRAPHY OF MARESHAH & MORESHETH GAT

Mareshah was located in the Guvrin Valley, the southern part of the Shephelah region that separated the Israelites from the Philistines. Mareshah is believed to have been a prominent city in the Guvrin Valley, being along a much-traveled route to Hebron. The prophet Micah was born in the neighboring town of Moresheth (cf. Mic. 1:1).

THE HISTORY OF MARESHAH & MORESHETH GAT

Following Judah's exile by the Babylonians, the Edomites took over Mareshah. After Alexander the Great's rapid rise and sudden death, the Seleucid Empire warred with the Ptolemaic Empire for control of Mareshah. Then, under the leadership of Judas Maccabeus, Jewish zealots took the city and destroyed it. Mareshah returned to the Edomites by the hand of the Roman ruler Pompey in 63 B.C. Sixteen years later, Julius Caesar apportioned Mareshah to Judea, and the city was ultimately destroyed seven years after that by the Parthians.[76]

THE ARCHAEOLOGY OF MARESHAH & MORESHETH GAT

Archaeological endeavors at Mareshah reveal three main periods in the city's history, only one of which is attributed to the time of the Israelites.[77] The other two are attributed to the Hellenistic periods. The artifacts dated to the time of Israelite inhabitation include a gallery of "rich pottery"[78] from the third and second centuries B.C. Others findings include gravesites and

QUICK FACTS

Mareshah was among the cities divided out to Judah during the conquest of Canaan.

Although the Bible records few details about the city, historians and archaeologists believe it was an important economic center for ancient Israel.

REFERENCES

Joshua 15:44

2 Chronicles 11:8; 14:9-10

Micah 1:15

---

76 Myers, et. al., *Eerdmans Dictionary of the Bible*, 856

77 Ibid. 857.

78 Ibid.

markings consistent with ancient tombs. The array and quality of artifacts found at Mareshah lead archaeologists to believe the city was economically significant in Israel.[79]

After the Nabateans drove out the Edomites, the Edomites settled in Judean towns, such a Mareshah, whose inhabitants were then exiled to Babylon. Clay tablets inscribed in Aramaic from the time of the Edomites occupation were discovered in Mareshah. Later, in the second century B.C., the Phoenicians occupied Mareshah, as evidenced by the discovery of "elaborate tombs belonging to a Sidonian family."[80] Mareshah is considered one of the foremost sites for showcasing the spread of Hellenistic influence in the second century B.C. Excavations revealed a thoroughly "Greek city," complete "with streets laid out on a grid of right angles" and houses built between streets.[81] Remains of a traditional Greek marketplace can also be seen next to the city gate.[82]

MARESHAH AND MORESHETH GAT IN THE BIBLE

Mareshah is site of Asa king of Judah's conflict with Zerah the Ethiopian (cf. 2 Chron. 14:9-10).[83] 2 Chronicles 14 describes Asa as one of those rare rulers who "did what was good and right in the eyes of the Lord his God" (14:2). After Asa secured and fortified Judah, enjoying years of peace, 2 Chronicles 14:9 says that Zerah the Ethiopian came out to attack Judah with an imposing force of "a million men and 300 chariots" (14:9), in comparison to Asa's army of 580,000 (cf. 2 Chron. 14:8).

It was at Mareshah where Asa and Judah faced the awe-inspiring threat of Zerah's army and where the Lord also answered Asa's prayer. The Lord "defeated the Ethiopians before Asa and before Judah" (14:12). Interestingly, Mareshah is also one of many cities whose destruction is specifically foretold by the prophet Micah in Micah 1:15 as a result of Judah's sin against the Lord, which took root in the people's heart despite the influence of righteous kings like Asa.

WHAT CAN WE LEARN FROM MARESHAH AND MORESHETH?

Interestingly, the small number of biblical references to Mareshah portray the bookends of Israel's time in the Promised Land as a sovereign nation:

....

79 Ibid.

80 Aaron P. Schade, "Ammonites, Moabites, Phoenicians, Arameans, and Edomites," ed. Kent P. Jackson, in *A Bible Reader's History of the Ancient World* (Provo, UT: Brigham Young University, 2016), 205.

81 John D. Currid and David P. Barrett, *ESV Bible Atlas* (Wheaton, IL: Crossway, 2010), 195

82 Ibid.

83 Myers, et. al., *Eerdmans Dictionary of the Bible.*

inheritance and exile. Joshua 15:44 records that Mareshah was given to the tribe of Judah as a city to settle and enjoy. Fast forward thousands of years to Micah 1:15 where the prophet Micah prophesied the destruction of Mareshah at the hand of the Babylonians as punishment for Judah's rampant and persistent unfaithfulness to the LORD. The first reference to Mareshah is one of hope and anticipation, the last one of doom and darkness. However, the prophet Micah later declared words of hope amidst the vast destruction based on God's unfailing character:

> *"Who is a God like you, pardoning iniquity and passing over transgression for the remnant of his inheritance? He does not retain his anger forever, because he delights in steadfast love. He will again have compassion on us; he will tread our iniquities underfoot. You will cast all our sins into the depths of the sea. You will show faithfulness to Jacob and steadfast love to Abraham, as you have sworn to our fathers from the days of old."*
>
> MICAH 7:18-20

When the story of our lives reads a little like the story of Mareshah, from great promise to great devastation, we, like the prophet Micah, can find hope and comfort in the unchanging love of our God. In Christ, we can embrace even the pain of discipline as a sign of His steadfast love and look toward the day of restoration and redemption (cf. Heb. 12:3-11; Rom. 8:23-25).

> *For in this hope we were saved. Now hope that is seen is not hope. For who hopes for what he sees? But if we hope for what we do not see, we await for it with patience.*
>
> ROMANS 8:24-25

MOUNT OF OLIVES
THE AGONY AND THE ECSTASY

"Men of Galilee," they said, "why do you stand here looking into the sky? This same Jesus, who has been taken from you into heaven, will come back in the same way you have seen him go into heaven."

ACTS 1:11

BACKGROUND, ARCHAEOLOGY AND SIGNIFICANCE:

BACKGROUND

The mountainous ridge called the Mount of Olives stretches from the Hebrew University Mount Scopus in the north, to the village of Silwan in the south. The olive gardens and olive press or "Gatshemen" in Hebrew, would have been located at the bottom of the mountain. The name "Gethsemane" comes from this Hebrew word.

Few places in the world are able to boast as many churches as the Mount of Olives. Virtually every Gospel event that occurred on the Mount is commemorated here. There is a small Arab village at the top of the mountain. The rest is inhabited only by these memorial churches.

THE ARCHAEOLOGY OF THE MOUNT OF OLIVES

According to Ezekiel 11, Zechariah 14, and Joel 3:2, the resurrection of the dead will begin in the Valley of Jehoshaphat (more commonly known as the Kidron Valley) at the foot of the Mount of Olives. Since Old Testament times, Jerusalemites have been buried on the slopes of the mountain. One such tomb near Silwan has been identified as belonging to Shebna, the scribe of King Hezekiah, mentioned in Isaiah 22:15-19. Another tomb in Silwan is said to belong to Isaiah.

The area of the Garden of Gethsemane has few archaeological remains since there are few structures to be found in a garden. The only evidence pointing its original function as an olive press are the channels, catchment basins, and a shallow pool cut into the rock in the Gethsemane Cave, east of the Tomb of Mary.

QUICK FACTS

The western slope has been covered with olive trees since the time of King David.

The Garden of Gethsemane would have been located at the foot of the mountain.

"Gethsemane" refers to the olive gardens and olive press.

REFERENCES

Ezekiel 11

Zechariah 14

Joel 3:2

2 Samuel 15:30

1 Kings 11:7-8

Zechariah 14:4

Luke 24:50-51

Matthew 26:36-56

THE MOUNT OF OLIVES IN THE OLD TESTAMENT

The soft limestone of the mountain is ideal for planting olive trees. By the time of King David, the western slope of the mountain was already covered with olive trees. When David's son Absalom led a revolt against his father, David and his family fled across the Kidron Valley and up the Mount of Olives:

> But David continued up the Mount of Olives, weeping as he went; his head was covered and he was barefoot. All the people with him covered their heads too and were weeping as they went up.
>
> 2 SAMUEL 15:30

After David's death, Solomon later built shrines for his foreign wives to worship their gods:

> On a hill east of Jerusalem, Solomon built a high place for Chemosh the detestable god of Moab, and for Molech the detestable god of the Ammonites. He did the same for all his foreign wives, who burned incense and offered sacrifices to their gods.
>
> 1 KINGS 11:7-8

THE MOUNT OF OLIVES IN THE NEW TESTAMENT

On more than one occasion, the Gospels record Jesus' sorrow for Jerusalem as he made his way down the slopes from the Mount of Olives. It was a path he would have known from childhood from his many visits to Jerusalem.

> "O Jerusalem, Jerusalem, you who kill the prophets and stone those sent to you, how often I have longed to gather your children together, as a hen gathers her chicks under her wings, but you were not willing! Look, your house is left to you desolate. I tell you, you will not see me again until you say, 'Blessed is he who comes in the name of the Lord.'"
>
> LUKE 13:34-35

Down the road from Bethphage, he came riding on a donkey colt with palm branches symbolic of Judaea strewn along the way. In the following week, Jesus passed this way several more times before celebrating Passover with his disciples.

After the Passover meal, Jesus and his disciples went to the Garden of Gethsemane at the foot of the mountain. Here, he prayed about his impending ordeal and for his disciples. He suffered agony as he prayed to be spared the crucifixion. It was here where Judas betrayed him with a kiss and the temple police arrested Jesus.

After the resurrection, Jesus parted from his disciples near Bethany, on the eastern side of the Mount of Olives (Luke 24:50- 51).

> He said to them: "It is not for you to know the times or dates the
> Father has set by his own authority. But you will receive power
> when the Holy Spirit comes on you; and you will be my witnesses in
> Jerusalem, and in all Judea and Samaria, and to the ends of the earth."
> After he said this, he was taken up before their very eyes, and a cloud
> hid him from their sight.
>
> ACTS 1:7-9

A few moments later, when the angels appeared to the disciples, they announced that Jesus would return in the same way that he left (Acts 1:11). This statement was a clear reference to Zechariah 14:4, the prophecy of Christ's return to the Mount of Olives.

A short time later, there was an attempted overthrow of the Roman occupation. An Egyptian false prophet led a sizable group down the Mount of Olives, intending to attack the Roman garrison at the Antonia. The Roman governor heard about the plan ahead of time and the insurrectionists were routed, but the leader was never caught. The Roman commander who later took Paul into custody on the Temple Mount thought that Paul was the Egyptian rebel who had returned (Acts 21:30-39).

THE OLIVE TREE

The olive tree was the most valuable and useful tree grown in Israel. The trees, which can reach a height of 20 feet, will grow for centuries if left undisturbed. If an olive tree is cut down, shoots will grow from the root, producing new trees.

Though some of the olive trees in the Garden of Gethsemane are ancient, none date to the time of Christ. When Jerusalem was destroyed in 70 A.D., General Titus ordered all Jerusalem's trees to be cut down.

Olive trees produce fruit in abundance. Olives and bread were staples in the ancient Israelite diet. In biblical times, olives from Israel were a major export to foreign markets. In Zechariah 4:3, the two olive trees in the prophetic vision were symbolic of the abundance with which God provided for the people, far beyond their needs.

Olive trees have a small white blossom, which can be easily blown off by the wind. Historically, when the olives were ready to be picked in November, tarps or blankets were spread below the trees. The branches were then shaken or beaten with poles. According to the Law, any remaining olives were left for the poor:

> *When you beat the olives from your trees, do not go over the branches*
> *a second time. Leave what remains for the alien, the fatherless and*
> *the widow.*

DEUTERONOMY 24:20

After being gathered from the tarps into baskets, the olives were brought to the place of pressing. The baskets would be stacked and crushed beneath the weight of a heavy stone. As the oil seeped out, it was strained through the numerous baskets and collected in a shallow stone basin. In biblical times, the initial crushing was sometimes done by the feet of harvesters in depressions found in the rock. The oil would then be poured into storage jars.

Not all olives are created equal. Cultivated olives are the best, while those from wild trees are relatively small and worthless. But like many fruit trees, olives can be grafted. When cultivated shoots are grafted onto a wild tree, the resulting tree becomes fruitful with large olives.

However, when the Apostle Paul used the olive tree as an analogy of the Gentile-Jewish relationship, the procedure was reversed: the wild branch is grafted onto the cultivated tree.

> *If some of the branches have been broken off, and you, though a wild*
> *olive shoot, have been grafted in among the others and now share in*
> *the nourishing sap from the olive root.*

ROMANS 11: 17

Paul was not ignorant of olive grafting. Instead, he reversed the image to demonstrate God's ability to change even a "worthless" branch into a fully fruitful branch. In the same way, the gentile Church is to rejoice in God's mercy for including them in the covenant of God's people.

WHAT CAN WE LEARN FROM THE MOUNT OF OLIVES?

THE CRUSHING OF THE OLIVE

Throughout the Bible, the olive tree is used in a variety of symbolic meanings. It was symbolic of the fruitful life of a righteous person:

> *But I am like an olive tree flourishing in the house of God; I trust in*
> *God's unfailing love for ever and ever.*
>
> PSALM 52:8

The olive tree was considered the most necessary and useful of all trees. In addition to food, olives provided oil for light, healing, and anointing.

In nearly all cases, for the olive to be useful, it had to be crushed. Gethsemane was the place where olives harvested from the mountain were crushed. In the Gospel story, Gethsemane was also the place where the Son of God was crushed. Like the olive, Jesus represented light, healing, and kingship. But to be effective at his mission, he had to be broken.

> *"My soul is overwhelmed with sorrow to the point of death. Stay here*
> *and keep watch with me." Going a little farther, he fell with his face*
> *to the ground and prayed, "My Father, if it is possible, may this cup be*
> *taken from me. Yet not as I will, but as you will."*
>
> MATTHEW 26:38-39

Jesus submitted to the crushing of his soul as he wrestled with God's will for him to die. It was in this garden that Jesus agonized over what he knew was in store for him, the suffering and shame for one who had never known sin, guilt, or shame.

Yes, Jesus' punishment for our sake began here at Gethsemane. But he would also be satisfied with the results of his suffering. He would ascend to heaven not very far away. As you stand here, meditate on Isaiah's prophecy. The light he saw was the light that you bear to the world in his name. Go forth and shine!

Who has believed what he has heard from us? And to whom has the arm of the Lord been revealed? For he grew up before him like a young plant, and like a root out of dry ground; he had no form or majesty that we should look at him, and no beauty that we should desire him. He was despised and rejected by men; a man of sorrows, and acquainted with grief; and as one from whom men hide their faces he was despised, and we esteemed him not.

> *Surely he has borne our griefs and carried our sorrows; yet we esteemed him stricken, smitten by God, and afflicted. But he was pierced for our transgressions; he was crushed for our iniquities; upon him was the chastisement that brought us peace, and with his wounds we are healed.*
>
> ISAIAH 53:1-5

> *Yet it was the will of the Lord to crush him; he has put him to grief; when his soul makes an offering for guilt, he shall see his offspring; he shall prolong his days; the will of the Lord shall prosper in his hand. Out of the anguish of his soul he shall see and be satisfied; by his knowledge shall the righteous one, my servant, make many to be accounted righteous, and he shall bear their iniquities. Therefore I will divide him a portion with the many, and he shall divide the spoil with the strong, because he poured out his soul to death and was numbered with the transgressors; yet he bore the sin of many, and makes intercession for the transgressors.*
>
> ISAIAH 53:10-12

JERUSALEM
THE HOLY CITY

Glorious things are said of you, O city of God...

PSALM 87:3

BACKGROUND, ARCHAEOLOGY AND SIGNIFICANCE:

THE HISTORY OF THE CITY OF JERUSALEM

The earliest settlers of Jerusalem lived near the Gihon spring about 3500 B.C. The first mention of the city is found in Egyptian execration texts, written on clay figurines in the 19th century B.C. (These figurines, after having written on them curses against rebels and foreign nations, would be smashed to the ground in hopes the enemies would suffer a similar fate.) At this time, Jerusalem was controlled by Egypt; the curse texts indicate the city was either in a state of rebellion or was making moves toward independence. Further evidence of Jerusalem's move away from Egypt is the presence of Canaanite city walls, a sign the inhabitants were preparing for a possible Egyptian military response.

During this period, the city was confined to the Ophel or the spur of the ridge that runs south of the Temple Mount. This is the general period in which Abraham met Melchizedek, the priest-king of Salem, as Jerusalem was then known:

> *And Melchizedek king of Salem brought*
> *out bread and wine. (He was priest of God*
> *Most High.)*
>
> GENESIS 14:18

When the Israelites entered the land centuries later, Jerusalem was ruled by the Canaanite king Adoni-Zedek.

> *As soon as Adoni-zedek, king of Jerusalem,*
> *heard how Joshua had captured Ai and*
> *had devoted it to destruction, doing to*
> *Ai and its king as he had done to Jericho*
> *and its king, and how the inhabitants of*

The earliest settlers of Jerusalem lived near the Gihon spring about 3500 B.C.

Jerusalem was previously known as Salem in the Old Testament.

The Ophel is the City of David, which is still considered part of Jerusalem.

The perimeter of the walls is just under two-and-a-half miles with an average wall height of 39.37 feet and average thickness is 8.2 feet. The walls contain 34 watchtowers and eight gates.

The Western Wall of the Temple Mount is considered one of the holiest sites in Judaism.

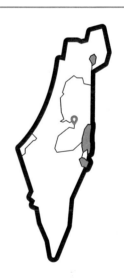

REFERENCES

Genesis 14:18

Joshua 15:8

2 Samuel 5:1-12

2 Kings 18:17 -19:37;
25:1-21

Ezra

Nehemiah

Psalm 87, 122, 125,
128, 137, 147

Acts 1-7

Gibeon had made peace with Israel and were among them, he feared greatly, because Gibeon was a great city, like one of the royal cities, and because it was greater than Ai, and all its men were warriors. So Adoni-zedek king of Jerusalem sent to Hoham king of Hebron, to Piram king of Jarmuth, to Japhia king of Lachish, and to Debir king of Eglon, saying, "Come up to me and help me, and let us strike Gibeon. For it has made peace with Joshua and with the people of Israel."

JOSHUA 10:1-4

Although the Israelites defeated this coalition, they did not capture Jerusalem at this time. The city, located near the boundary of the tribal allotments of Judah and Benjamin, remained under Canaanite control.

David conquered the walled city on the Ophel ridge in about 1004 B.C. (2 Samuel 5:6-8). He chose Jerusalem as the capital of a united Israel. Its central location, as well as the fact that it had not yet been occupied by Israelites, made it a suitable capital for all the tribes. The "City of David", as the area of the original city was thereafter known, became the political and religious capital of all the tribes of Israel. David built his palace there, and the Ark of the Covenant was transferred to a temporary location within the city.

King Solomon expanded Jerusalem northward to include the threshing floor of Araunah, the present-day Temple Mount. In addition to this expansion, he also beautified the city with several buildings. These included Solomon's palace, which took 13 years to build and was located just south of the Temple Mount. The Temple, built on the threshing floor of Araunah, took seven years to construct and was completed around 969 B.C.

Jerusalem warded off several threats of invasion over the next few centuries, first by the Philistines, and later by the Egyptians under Pharaoh Shishak (924 B.C.).

Although Jerusalem came under attack from the Assyrians in 701 B.C. during the reign of Hezekiah, the city was miraculously spared (2 Kings 18-19).

Nebuchadnezzar, King of Babylon, finally succeeded in destroying Jerusalem and the Temple in 586 B.C. Most of the population was deported to Babylon; it was not until Cyrus, King of Persia, conquered the Babylonians that Jews were allowed to return to their land. The return began in 538 B.C. under Zerubbabel, the first governor of Judah after the exile; the Temple was rebuilt under Ezra in 515 B.C. The old city walls, destroyed in the Babylonian conquest, remained as piles of rubble until Nehemiah led the people to rebuild them in 445 B.C.

Jerusalem continued under Persian rule until the time of Alexander the Great. The city, along with the rest of the region, began to be influenced by Hellenization as well as the politics of Alexander's successors. The policy of Hellenization was the process of incorporating Greek culture, language and religion; Hellenization became an oppressive force in Israel during the reign of Antiochus IV Epiphanes, who ruled from Syria. In 169 B.C. Antiochus IV Epiphanes attacked and plundered Jerusalem, profaned the Temple, and outlawed the practice of Judaism. It was this move that sparked a Jewish revolt under the leadership of the Hasmonean family, a revolt that led to Jewish independence in 165 B.C. The Temple was rededicated, and Israel became an independent nation for the first time since the Babylonian exile four centuries before.

The Hasmonean (also known as Maccabean) family continued ruling from Jerusalem, although their rule became increasingly marked by corruption. Jewish self-rule effectively ended when the Roman general Pompey conquered Jerusalem in 63 B.C. Herod the Great was installed by the Roman Senate as king in 40 B.C. and began his rule (under Roman protection) in Jerusalem in 37 B.C. To ingratiate himself with his subjects, Herod had the Temple and the surrounding area rebuilt at his expense in a manner and scale that attracted the admiration of the world. The Roman natural historian Pliny the Elder called Jerusalem "...by far the most renowned city of the ancient East" (Natural History 5.14). The city increased in size considerably during Herod's rule, spreading to the north and northwest to an area of about 450 acres. Herod also built a palace on the western side of the city near what is now called Jaffa Gate.

Jerusalem remained under the control of the Herodian royal family until A.D. 44, when the Romans decided to rule it directly. The First Jewish Revolt against Roman occupation began in A.D. 66. Four years later, the siege of Jerusalem ended with the destruction of the city and the Temple, as well as the annihilation or slavery of the entire population.

Although Jerusalem was gradually repopulated, it participated in yet another uprising against Rome, the Bar Kokhba revolt of A.D. 135. Not only was the city destroyed again, but its inhabitants were expelled, and Jews were forbidden to return. The Roman Emperor Hadrian took the opportunity to rebuild Jerusalem as a pagan Roman city, renaming it Aelia Capitolina. The city continued under Roman and then Byzantine rule until the seventh century, when it fell to the Muslims.

THE LAYOUT OF JERUSALEM

The city of Jerusalem is located in the Judean hills about 2,600 feet above sea level. The modern city is divided into two parts, the Old City (the area surrounded by the walls) and the New City (everywhere outside the walls). The current city walls are not the same as those Jesus would have seen, nor are they necessarily on the same line as the earlier walls. The length of the walls is 4,018 meters (2.4966 miles) with an average height of 12meters (39.37 feet) and the average thickness is 2.5 meters (8.2 feet). The walls contain 34 watchtowers and eight gates, two of which are sealed. The Old City is divided into four quarters: Jewish, Armenian, Christian, and Muslim. The names of these quarters reflect the makeup of the population that has historically lived in the areas. The Jerusalem of Jesus' day was spread over several ridges running north to south.

THE WESTERN WALL

Located in the Old City of Jerusalem at the foot of the western side of the Temple Mount is the Western Wall. It is a remnant of the ancient wall that surrounded the Jewish Temple's courtyard. This part of the wall is arguably the most sacred site recognized by the Jewish faith outside of the Temple Mount itself. Just over half the wall, including its 17 courses located below street level, dates from the end of the Second Temple period. This section of the wall was allegedly built around 19 B.C. by Herod the Great, but some excavations indicate the works were not finished during Herod's lifetime.

This wall acts as a retaining wall to support Herod's massive construction on the Second Temple. In building and reconstructing the Second Temple, Herod leveled the top of Mt. Moriah and constructed large foundation stones to support the entire area of the Temple Mount. These foundation stones are extraordinary as they are immense in size and constructed of one whole stone rather than brick and mortar. The Western Wall is one of the retaining walls to hold up the entire Temple Mount, exemplifying Herod's extraordinary vision for constructing large and impressive structures. One of the largest stones, seen below, is 41 feet long, 11.5 feet high and 15 feet wide, as large as a school bus. This is one solid stone and estimated to weigh up to 630 tons or 1.2 million pounds and baffles engineers to this day as to how they moved it into place.

THE WESTERN WALL TUNNELS

Located underground adjacent the Western Wall, there are tunnels that reveal the vast foundational structures which support the retaining walls to the entire Temple Mount.

In the nineteenth century, the most distinguished Jerusalem scholars were already trying to determine the precise measurements of the Western Wall and describe the methods used in its construction. However, their information was incomplete, mainly because they were unable to discover the wall's entire length. Nevertheless, British researchers Charles Wilson, in 1864 and Charles Warren, in 1867-1870, uncovered the northern extension of the Western Wall Prayer Plaza. The shafts that Charles Warren dug through Wilson's Arch can still be seen today.

Immediately after the Six Day War, the Ministry of Religious Affairs began the project of exposing the entire length of the Western Wall.

It was a difficult operation, which involved digging beneath residential neighborhoods that had been constructed on ancient structures from the Second Temple period and were built up against the Western Wall. Some residents used underground spaces as water holes or for sewage collection. The excavations required close supervision by experts in the fields of structural engineering, securing subterranean tunnels, archeology, and of course, Jewish Law.

After almost twenty years, and despite enormous difficulties, the Western Wall Tunnels were excavated. This lengthy project unearthed many archaeological finds, which can only be described as remarkable. These finds revealed new and unknown details about the history and the geography of the Temple Mount site.

When the Western Wall Heritage Foundation was established, it was given the responsibility of continuing the excavations, which revealed ancient Jerusalem in all its glory, and bringing them to the public's attention by opening the tunnels to visitors.

ROBINSON ARCH

The Robinson Arch is located outside the Davidson Center, southwest of the Temple Mount. Robinson's Arch is the name given to an arch that once stood at the southwestern corner of the Temple Mount. It was built during the reconstruction of the Second Temple initiated by Herod the Great at the end of the first century B.C. The massive stone span was constructed along with the retaining walls of the Temple Mount. It carried traffic up from ancient Jerusalem's lower market area and over the Tyropoeon street to the Royal Stoa complex on the esplanade of the Mount. The overpass was destroyed during the Great Jewish Revolt, only a few decades after its completion.

The arch is named after Biblical scholar Edward Robinson who identified its remnants in 1838. Excavations during the second half of the 20th century revealed both its purpose and the extent of its associated structures. Today the public within the Jerusalem Archaeological Park may view the considerable surviving portions of the ancient overpass complex.

SOUTHERN WALL STAIRS

Outside of the ancient walls of Jerusalem are the southern steps, which served as a major entrance point into the ancient city. Located around these steps are ancient ritual baths called Mikvehs, which were used for purity baths before entering the Holy City.

The Southern Wall is 922 feet in length. Herod's southern extension of the Temple Mount is clearly visible from the east, standing on the Mount of Olives or to a visitor standing on top of the Temple mount as a slight change in the plane of the eastern wall, the so-called "Straight Joint." Herod's Royal Stoa stood atop this southern extension. The enormous retaining wall is built of enormous blocks of Jerusalem stone, the face of each ashlar (block) is edged with a margin, the boss is raised about 3/8" above the surrounding margins. The unmortared blocks are so finely fitted together that a knife blade cannot be inserted between the ashlars.

The Southern Stairs were excavated after 1967 by archaeologist Benjamin Mazar and are the northernmost extension of the Jerusalem pilgrim road leading from the Pool of Siloam to the Temple Mount via the Double Gate and the Triple Gate, collectively called the Huldah Gates. These are the steps that Jesus and other Jews of His era walked up to approach the Temple, especially on the great pilgrimage festivals of Passover, Shavuot and Sukkot. Many believe that Jesus frequently taught on these very steps, as did many other Rabbis during the time. These steps are also referred to as the Rabbis Teaching Stairway and connect the Ophel (City of David) to the Southern end of the Temple Mount.

THE HISTORICAL GEOGRAPHY OF JERUSALEM

The earliest settlement was near the Gihon Spring at the foot of the City of David spur. This spring provided enough water for the City of David, with some additional supply from rainwater collected in cisterns. Another spring near the city is En-Rogel, located south of the Gihon spring in the Kidron Valley.

The early inhabitants of the city were farmers and shepherds. Olives, figs, and grapes grow well in this hill country, but grain must have been grown far outside the city. Vegetables and fruit could be grown in the Kidron Valley near the Gihon Spring.

The size of the city has waxed and waned, depending upon the political and religious fortunes of the day. The Canaanite city occupied only about 12 acres; after the Israelite capital was established in Jerusalem, the city experienced considerable growth. The population swelled with an influx of pilgrims coming for the festivals several times a year, with administrative and military leaders, and with craftsmen for building projects.

By the time Solomon extended the city to include the Temple Mount, it had expanded to 32 acres. By the reign of Hezekiah (about 700 BC) Jerusalem had quadrupled in size to about 125 acres, expanding onto the Western Hill (now the Jewish Quarter). This expansion was necessary in order to house refugees from the conquered Northern Kingdom, as well as other Jews fleeing from the Assyrian invasions in the west.

With the Babylonian destruction of the city in 586 B.C., most of the population of Jerusalem was taken into captivity. The return to the city began under Ezra and Nehemiah, although the inhabited area was probably limited to the confines of the original city of David. The city grew slowly, but by the time of Jesus it was about 250 acres. Its prosperity depended heavily upon Jewish pilgrimage for the festivals, patronage by the Herodian royal family, and the Temple tax paid by every Jewish male whether living in Jerusalem or not.

THE ARCHAEOLOGY OF JERUSALEM

While many tourists assume that Jerusalem must be an archaeologist's paradise, it is actually more of a nightmare. In the first place, the city has been almost continually inhabited for over 5,000 years; the fact that it is still inhabited means most of the area is not available for excavation.

Another difficulty is that after each of its seventeen destructions, the city was rebuilt, reusing old foundations or stones robbed from ruined buildings. The state of preservation of buildings from biblical times is therefore quite poor.

The hilly terrain also affects the archaeology. When buildings at the top of a hill collapsed, they would tumble down into the valleys, taking other structures with them in an avalanche of stone. As the valleys became filled with the devastation of proceeding ages, the reconstruction of original buildings – or even building layouts – is next to impossible in many cases.

The Second Temple Model of the City of Jerusalem (The Israel Museum)

One of the best ways to become acquainted with the city is to visit the scale model (1:50) of the city, located on the grounds of The Israel Museum. It was originally built at the initiative of Holy Land Hotel owner Hans Kroch in memory of his son Jacob, who fell in Israel's War of Independence. It is called the Second Temple Model because it represents the city as it looked when the Second Temple (the one largely rebuilt by Herod the Great) was still standing before its destruction in AD 70. The model has been constructed from the same materials as the original buildings. Designed by an archaeologist, the late Professor Avi-Yonah, the model was constructed by artist R. Brotzen. As excavations continue, the model is updated to reflect the new knowledge. In 2006 the Second Temple Model was moved to the Israel Museum.

As you view the model for the first time, notice the basic topography of the city. Notice that the city slopes downward toward the south where the valleys of the Hinnom (the sidewalk near the entrance), the Tyropaean (in front of the Temple platform), and the Kidron meet. The part of the city first inhabited is the lowest part of the city, the City of David, near the Gihon Spring.

Note that there are several walls around the city. Herod rebuilt the walls along the line of the older walls from Old Testament times, as well as expanding them to the north and west. He also built three impressive towers, placed in the area on the west near Jaffa Gate, in memory of his favorite wife Mariamne (whom he killed), his brother Phasael, and his friend Hippicus. A second wall fortified the small area from his palace (near Jaffa Gate) to the Damascus Gate. It was just outside this second wall that Jesus was crucified on Calvary. In the model you will notice Calvary or Golgotha as a small hill just outside the second (middle) wall. The third wall, built after the time of Christ by Herod Agrippa I, included the large suburb, which had spread to the north.

DAVID IN JERUSALEM

ISRAEL'S FIRST HOLY CITY

Surely no prophet can die outside Jerusalem!

LUKE 13:33

BACKGROUND, ARCHAEOLOGY AND SIGNIFICANCE:

FIRST IMPRESSIONS

The ancient city conquered by David may seem much smaller than one would have imagined. It is hard to believe that the "city of the great king" could fit on the small tongue shaped piece of land south of the Temple Mount, limited by the Kidron and Tyropaean valleys.

The ridge slopes upwards from south to north, with the Temple Mount an extension of the City of David. The area of the City of David now lies outside the city wall built by the Turkish Sultan Suleiman the Magnificent (A.D. 1539-42). It is currently a residential area with homes built over the rubble of thousands of years of habitation (excavations are happening under these homes). An extensive area on the eastern slope of the city has been excavated, revealing ancient city walls dating back to the time of King David and earlier.

THE CITY OF DAVID IN THE OLD TESTAMENT

After defeating the kings that had invaded Sodom and Gomorrah, Abraham received food and a blessing from Melchizedek, King of Salem and priest of God Most High (Genesis 14:18-20). Salem is most likely to be identified with Jerusalem, and it is the first mention of the city in the Bible.

The next mention of Jerusalem is during the campaigns of Joshua. He fought Adoni-Zedek, King of Jerusalem, along with four other kings who opposed the Israelites' entry into the land (Joshua 10:1-27). While Adoni-Zedek and the others were defeated, Jerusalem remained unconquered until the time of David.

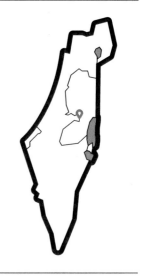

REFERENCES

Genesis 14:18-20

2 Samuel 5:6-10; 6:16-7:29; 11:1-12:25

1 Kings 1:28—53

2 Kings 14:13-14; 19:32-34

1 Chronicles 11:4-7

2 Chronicles 32:30

Nehemiah 3:15

Isaiah 7:3; 22:9, 11; 29:1-8

Luke 13:4-5

John 9:1-12

Acts 2:29

David's capture of city is described in 2 Samuel 5:

> *And the king and his men went to Jerusalem against the Jebusites,*
> *the inhabitants of the land, who said to David, "You will not come in*
> *here, but the blind and the lame will ward you off "—thinking, "David*
> *cannot come in here." Nevertheless, David took the stronghold of Zion,*
> *that is, the city of David.*

2 SAMUEL 5:6-7

David took the city by entering through the 'conduit', probably the water tunnel. Once taken, the city became the capital of the united Kingdom of Israel. David built a palace there; and although he desired to build a temple for the Lord, that project remained for his son Solomon.

It was from the roof of David's palace, probably on high ground toward the north, that David saw Bathsheba bathing. In his palace Nathan the prophet rebuked David for his adultery with Bathsheba and his murder of Uriah the Hittite. The court intrigue of David's family, with David's sons vying for power, all took place within the confines of the small yet fortified City of David. It was within the city that David was buried, as was most of the royal family thereafter.

During the reign of Hezekiah, the Assyrian king Sennacherib advanced down the coast of Israel and threatened Jerusalem in 701 B.C. Hezekiah responded to the threat by digging a tunnel to bring the water supply within the walls of the city and by building larger walls and extra reservoirs for water. He prayed to God for the city to be spared:

> *And Hezekiah prayed before the Lord and said: "O Lord, the God of*
> *Israel, enthroned above the cherubim, you are the God, you alone, of*
> *all the kingdoms of the earth; you have made heaven and earth. Incline*
> *your ear, O Lord, and hear; open your eyes, O Lord, and see; and hear*
> *the words of Sennacherib, which he has sent to mock the living God.*
> *Truly, O Lord, the kings of Assyria have laid waste the nations and*
> *their lands and have cast their gods into the fire, for they were not*
> *gods, but the work of men's hands, wood and stone. Therefore they*
> *were destroyed. So now, O Lord our God, save us, please, from his*
> *hand, that all the kingdoms of the earth may know that you, O Lord,*
> *are God alone."*

2 KINGS 19:15-19

In response to Hezekiah's prayer, God struck dead most of the Assyrian army dead overnight, and the city was spared.

Jerusalem would not be so fortunate in 586 B.C. when the Babylonians invaded. They utterly destroyed the city, including the Temple, deporting the people to Babylon. Under the leadership of Zerubbabel, Ezra, and Nehemiah, many Jews gradually returned to Jerusalem with the permission of the Persian rulers. Nehemiah's ride around Jerusalem to assess the damage to the walls, related in Nehemiah 2:12-16, is perhaps the best ancient source in identifying the ancient walls and gates of the city. Under his leadership the walls were rebuilt, and people once again built their houses in the area of the city of David.

THE CITY OF DAVID IN THE NEW TESTAMENT

One of the few mentions of the area of the city of David in the New Testament is the healing of the blind man in John 9:1-12. Jesus anointed the man's eyes with mud and told him to go wash in the Pool of Siloam at the southern end of the City of David. David's Tomb was also located in the area of the City of David and was mentioned by Peter (Acts 2:29) as a landmark that existed in his day (although most certainly, the Babylonian destruction would have destroyed any monument and robbed anything in the tomb).

THE ARCHAEOLOGY OF THE CITY OF DAVID

The fertile ground around the Spring of Gihon attracted settlers as early as the 4th millennium BC. The city was walled around 1800 B.C. to include the ridge of the City of David. Archaeologists have excavated 25 occupational levels of the city, representing periods from the earliest settlement to the medieval era.

Among the most interesting remains are the water systems, which include Warren's Shaft (named after the discoverer), the Siloam Channel, and Hezekiah's Tunnel.

The earliest system, Warren's Shaft, was a stepped tunnel leading to a place where jugs could be lowered down about 45 feet to a small pool. A horizontal channel brought the water from the spring to the pool. If the vertical shaft was the "conduit" through which David's men climbed to get into the city, it was a remarkable feat. The vertical shaft, about six feet wide, would have made the ascent extremely difficult. During the excavation, it took professional mountain climbers to get up the shaft.

If you visit the area of the City of David excavations, you will also see what appears to be a stepped stone structure 58 feet high and 52 feet wide. The date of the structure is the tenth century BC and must have been part of David's or Solomon's building projects. It is probably the retaining wall for the royal buildings (such as the house of the Forest of Lebanon, Solomon's palace, the palace for Pharaoh's daughter, etc.). The millo (2 Samuel 5:9) may be the "fill" in this area between the City of David and the Temple Mount, held in place by this massive wall.

During the excavations of Weill in 1923-24, an inscription by Theodotus was found regarding the donation of a synagogue and an adjoining hostel. Hostels were needed to house the Jewish pilgrims who came up to Jerusalem from their homelands from the Atlantic Ocean to the Euphrates River. The pilgrimage festivals drew perhaps as many as 100,000 visitors each. Unfortunately, there are not any remains of the synagogue of Theodotos or its hostels. If some of the buildings were preserved, it might have been possible to ascertain if this was the synagogue of Freedmen mentioned in Acts 6:9.

Some artifacts, assumed to be from the city of David, were turn up in private collections. These include a ring containing a seal belong to Hanan, the son of Hilkiah (2 Kings 22:8 and 2 Chronicles 34:14). There are also numerous clay bullae (small lumps of clay used to seal the name of Baruch, the son of Neriah, and Jerahmeel, the son of King Jehoiakim. The artifacts provide important connections to the life of the prophet Jeremiah. Baruch, describe of Jeremiah, undoubtedly lived in Jerusalem, where he twice wrote down Jeremiahs prophecies beginning in about 605 B.C. It is likely that all these discoveries come from the city of David. Unfortunately, the precise locations of theses discoveries are unknown.

HEZEKIAH'S TUNNEL AND THE POOL OF SILOAM

Located within the area of the City of David, Hezekiah's Tunnel was constructed during the reign of Hezekiah (715-687 B.C.), brought water from the Gihon Spring, and flowed south to the Pool of Siloam. Furthermore, 2 Chronicles 32:2-5 tell the story of Sennacherib's siege on Jerusalem and described Hezekiah and his men stoppering the flow of water from the Gihon Spring upon hearing of Sennacherib's intent on attacking Jerusalem. He said,

"Why should the king of Assyria come and find much water?"

At the south end of Hezekiah's tunnel near the Pool of Siloam is a Hebrew inscription, commonly named the Siloam Inscription, which says,

> "...the tunnel ... and this is the story of the tunnel while ... the axes were against each other and while three cubits were left to cut? ... the voice of a man ... called to his counterpart, (for) there was ZADA in the rock, on the right ... and on the day of the tunnel (being finished) the stonecutters struck each man towards his counterpart, ax against ax and flowed water from the outlet to the pool for 1200 cubits and 100 cubits was the height over the head of the stonecutters ..."

This inscription does not specifically state that Hezekiah constructed the tunnel however it is believed that this tunnel's construction was during King Hezekiah's reign. The inscription refers to an "outlet," which undoubtedly refers to the Gihon Spring and flowed to a "pool" likely referring to the Pool of Siloam.

There were likely other channels and pools that were located throughout the Kidron Valley prior to Hezekiah stopping the Gihon Springs in preparation for Sennacherib. Upon stoppering the spring, they dried up the entire Kidron Valley causing the Assyrian army from quenching their thirst.

Hezekiah also constructed a double wall to the east of the City of David to prevent Sennacherib and his forces from entering the city (2 Chronicles 32:5). Located near the Pool of Siloam is the Fountain or Spring Gate, which is likely where King Zedekiah fled Jerusalem to Arabah (Jer. 39:4; 2 Kings 25:4) when Nebuchadnezzar the king of Babylon besieged it. This gate is also referenced in Nehemiah 3:15 and Nehemiah 2:14 and describes Nehemiah repairing the "wall of the irrigation pool of the King's Garden."

Hezekiah's tunnel is accessible to the public today and can be seen walking through the tunnel starting near the Gihon Springs and exiting near the Pool of Siloam.

As King Hezekiah prepared the city to withstand the imminent Assyrian siege, he decided to bring the water supply into the city in a way that could not be cut off by the enemy outside the walls. To do this he sealed up the outward flow of the Gihon spring and dug a tunnel 1732 feet long, bringing the water into a pool called the pool of Siloam. An inscription, discovered in 1880 in the tunnel, describes the process of the tunneling.

The Gospel according to John describes Jesus healing a blind man at the Pool of Siloam (John 9:7) by putting a mudpack on his on his eyes and telling him to "Go, wash in the Pool of Siloam."

What you see today as the Pool of Siloam is only one of two pools in the area. The upper Pool of Siloam dates to about 701 B.C. By the time of Jesus, there was a covered porch at the entrance supported by six columns, and the pool itself was about four times the size of what you see today. The original pool of the Jebusites, called "the Shiloah" or "the sender," was outside the walls and further down the Tyropean Valley. This area is now a garden about sixty feet from the upper Pool of Siloam.

WHAT CAN WE LEARN FROM THE CITY OF DAVID?

HEZEKIAH'S PRELUDE TO PRAYER

What do you do when you're facing impossible situation?

Hezekiah did what most of us do: he got busy. While the Bible indicates numerous ways he prepared for the onslaught of the Assyrian army, archaeology supplements out knowledge about the extent of these preparations. He strengthened his defensive network of forts in the Shephelah (the lower rolling hills west of Jerusalem). He built huge towers to guard the gateways of key cities in his fortification network. Hezekiah established four supply depots and had storage jars made with special inscriptions on the handle ("For the King") for gathering supplies into the depots. And made an alliance with Egypt, hoping its army would come to rescue—but he did not pray.

> *"Ah, stubborn children," declares the Lord, "Who carry out a plan, but*
> *not mine, and who make an alliance, but not of my Spirit, that they*
> *may add sin to sin; who set out to go down to Egypt, without asking*
> *for my direction, to take refuge in the protection of Pharaoh and to*
> *seek shelter in the shadow of Egypt!"*
>
> ISAIAH 30:1-2

To strengthen the defensive capabilities of Jerusalem, Hezekiah blocked up the outer entrance to the Gihon Spring; he then had workers tunnel through the hill on which the City of David was built in order to bring the water within the wall area of the city. He also built additional reservoirs for water. He can and private houses in order to build a massive wall to defend the newer areas of the city– but he did not pray.

"…and you counted the houses of Jerusalem, and you broke down the
houses to fortify the wall. You made a reservoir between the two walls
for the water of the old pool. But you did not look to him who did it, or
see him who planned it long ago."

ISAIAH 22:10-11

Hezekiah even paid a bribe to Sennacherib, the king of Assyria, asking him to leave the cities of Judah alone. Hezekiah's bribe took gold from the house of the Lord as well as from the treasury—but he did not pray.

And Hezekiah king of Judah sent to the king of Assyria at Lachish,
saying, "I have done wrong; withdraw from me. Whatever you impose
on me I will bear." And the king of Assyria required of Hezekiah king
of Judah three hundred talents of silver and thirty talents of gold. And
Hezekiah gave him all the silver that was found in the house of the
Lord and in the treasuries of the king's house.

2 KINGS 18:14-15

Assyian messengers arrived to tell the Jews to surrender rather than to listen to Hezekiah or trust in God. Hezekiah, utterly distraught, sent for Isaiah and asked him to pray.

It may be that the Lord your God will hear all the words of the field
commander, whom his master, the king of Assyria, has sent to ridicule
the living God, and that he will rebuke him for the words the Lord your
God has heard. Therefore pray for the remnant that still survives.

2 KINGS 19:4

Note that Hezekiah referred to the Lord as Isaiah's God. He asked someone else to pray, but he did not pray.

Finally, Hezekiah took the enemy's letter demanding his surrender and went to the Temple. He spread the letter out before the Lord—and he prayed. He finally put the matter before God, and God answered him.

Therefore this is what the Lord says concerning the King of Assyria: He will not enter this city or shoot an arrow here. He will not come before it with shield or build a siege ramp against it. By the way that he came he will return; he will not enter this city, declares the Lord.

I will defend this city and save it, for my sake and for the sake of David
my servant."

2 KINGS 19:32-34

God decimated the Assyrian army, and the remnant retreated home to Nineveh. God accomplished what the king could not do, but God waited for Hezekiah to pray.

Is prayer our last resort, or our first response? Do we wait until the situation is truly out of our control, or do we trust God enough to ask his help from the beginning? Prayer is a matter of daily life, not of desperation alone:

> *Do not be anxious about anything, but in everything, by prayer and*
> *petition, with thanksgiving, present your requests to God. And the*
> *peace of God, which transcends all understanding, will guard your*
> *hearts and your minds in Christ Jesus.*

PHILIPPIANS 4:6-7

JESUS IN JERUSALEM

THE OLD CITY FOUND NEW LIFE

.

Surely no prophet can die outside Jerusalem!

LUKE 13:33

BACKGROUND, ARCHAEOLOGY AND SIGNIFICANCE:

FIRST IMPRESSIONS

Walls of honey-colored stones varying in size and shape confine the narrow streets and alleys of the Old City. The vendors, rapidly wheeling merchandise on carts down these alleyways, nearly run over the tourists, many of whom are standing transfixed in the time warp into which they feel they have entered.

This is not what most people imagine the holy city would look like; the remains from Jesus' day are usually several feet below the present street level. Many Christian pilgrims, oblivious of this fact, kneel and kiss the stones of the streets anyway – streets trod by Arab women from the villages who have brought their vegetables to market; orthodox Jews with their prayer shawls going to the Wall to pray; merchants, shoppers, soldiers, priests.

For many Christians, especially from the United States, the Church of the Holy Sepulchre is a particularly unexpected sight. How could this building possibly be the right place? The enormity of the building, the heavily ornamented shrines with their colorful candles and images, the fragmentation among the competing communities of faith, the disharmony of chants in different languages. Where is the hill of Calvary, the quiet tomb, the garden where Mary Magdalene brought spices for Jesus' body? Why are the places associated with the death of the Lord not like we always imagined they would be?

We often expect the locations of the crucifixion and resurrection, events that changed the course of history and of our lives, to have been kept in their pristine condition, or at least to have been returned to their original appearance. What we can fail to appreciate is that we are witnessing

REFERENCES

Matthew 26:20-35; 27:11 - 28:10

Mark 14:16-31; 15 - 16

Luke 22:13-38; 23:1-24:12; 24:36-49

John 5:1-18; 13 17; 19 20

Acts 1:12-2:41

the ways – sincere and with great devotion—that Christians of other cultures have expressed their worship of the Lord through the centuries.

Other changes have occurred as well. Since Jerusalem has continued to be inhabited, the city has undergone many changes over the centuries, just as any city would. Buildings have come and gone, the landscape of the area has been altered, the old has often been erased or buried. When we gaze down into the bottom of the excavations at the Pool of Bethesda, for example, we realize how much the topography of the city has changed, filling up valleys and pools with the debris that results from twenty centuries of human habitation.

People come here looking for the transcendent; they find the ordinary. Looking for solemnity, they find a hurried, working world. Looking for the eternal, they find the temporal. Yet in the person of Jesus, God's holiness came into intimate contact with this ordinary, hurried, temporal place in a way that changed the world forever.

THE EVENTS OF JESUS' LIFE IN JERUSALEM

Several events of Jesus' life happened here in this part of the city. In the western area, for example, was Herod's palace, where the king received the Magi who were inquiring about the birth of the one born King of the Jews.

After this there was a feast of the Jews, and Jesus went up to Jerusalem.

> *Now there is in Jerusalem by the Sheep Gate a pool, in Aramaic called Bethesda, which has five roofed colonnades.*
>
> JOHN 5:1-2

The first mention of Jesus visiting this area of the city is associated with a healing at the pools of Bethesda. The name, probably deriving from the Hebrew for "House of Mercy" (beth-hesedah), may indicate that there was a building by that name; in any event, the twin pools were also known as the Sheep Pool. Near this spot the paralytic was healed; one of the pools can be seen near St. Anne's Church.

Although the specific location of the upper room, the location of the Last Supper, is not given in the gospels, it would also have been in this area of the city. Traditionally, the location of the upper room is in the Armenian Quarter. It was in the upper room that Jesus celebrated Passover and instituted the Lord's Supper. Here also the apostles elected a replacement for Judas and received the Holy Spirit on the day of Pentecost (Acts 1:12-2:4).

After his condemnation by Pilate, Jesus was led out of the city to a hill called Calvary or Golgotha, where he was crucified. After his death, Jesus' body was laid in a new tomb owned by Joseph of Arimathea, a tomb apparently near the place of crucifixion. Traditionally, the Church of the Holy Sepulchre has been identified as the location for both the crucifixion and the tomb.

THE ARCHAEOLOGY OF JESUS' LIFE IN JERUSALEM THE POOLS OR BETHESDA (THE SHEEP POOL)

Part of the area of the twin pools associated with the healing of the paralytic has been excavated in the yard of the Church of St. Anne. The pools can still be seen in the northwest and northeast corners of the excavation trench. A dam separating the two pools carried a street across to what may have been the "house of mercy" associated with healing. The columns of the Byzantine church may have been reused from the original colonnades mentioned in John 5:2. A pagan sanctuary was built over the area in A.D. 135, which, oddly enough, confirms the location: small offerings found in the area identify the pagan structure as a healing sanctuary. Christians in the middle of the fifth century AD built their church over the remains of this sanctuary.

THE CHURCH OF THE HOLY SEPULCHRE

Although the Church of the Holy Sepulchre is now within the city walls, it was outside the walls of Jesus' day. Various places within the church contain remains from the first century, adding credibility to its identification as the location of Calvary and the empty tomb. Up the stairs you will see bedrock at a considerable height above the current floor; this is all that remains of the outcrop of rock, which is a probable location of Calvary.

Hadrian built a temple to the goddess Aphrodite directly over this outcrop of rock in A.D. 135. When the pagan temple was razed in A.D. 326, the workmen looked for the tomb of Christ. When they believed they had found the correct one, they dug out the bedrock around the tomb so that it now resembles a small chapel.

Next to a chapel claimed by the Armenians and the Syrians you will have access to several "kokhim", deep horizontal niches used in first-century graves. This area can therefore at least be identified as a place where first century tombs were located outside the city walls, and this being a possibility for the correct location of Jesus' tomb.

THE GARDEN TOMB

The Garden Tomb is an alternate location for the death and burial of Jesus Christ however this location is highly contested. The Garden Tomb was discovered in 1883 by the British General Charles Gordon who believe that a stone outcropping reminded him of what he believed Calvary should look like as well as a tomb nearby. However this tomb dates several years before the 1st century AD and Jesus was said to have been buried in a new tomb according to Luke 23:53, "a tomb cut in stone, where no one had ever yet been laid." Were it not for the New Testament statement that Joseph's tomb was new, this would not make this site such a controversial possibility.

The Garden Tomb, located north of Damascus Gate, was suggested in the 19th century as an alternative site of Calvary and Jesus' tomb. While the setting is very suggestive of what the garden would have looked like in the time of Jesus, excavations would seem to indicate that the tomb is too ancient to have been the one built by Joseph of Arimathea. The details of the chiseled walls and the bench type of arrangement suggest a date during the Old Testament.

Nonetheless, this is a very special place for more visiting believers today as they reflect on what it may have been like for Jesus to be crucified outside the city and then buried in a tomb near Jerusalem.

THE PALACE OF HEROD THE GREAT

Herod's palace was located in the area that is now called the Armenian Quarter of the Old City. The palace complex extended from David's Citadel to the area of Christ Church, the Jaffa Gate police station, and the Armenian Garden. Traces of the palace foundations, columns, and cisterns have been found in those areas. The foundations of the large tower inside Jaffa Gate are probably those of the tower of Phasael, which was built in memory of Herod's brother.

THE ROOM OF THE LAST SUPPER

The Cenacle, the traditional location of the upper room that Jesus borrowed in order to have Passover with his disciples, is in the area of the so-called "Tomb of David." (More correctly, the tomb was probably the royal burial place of the later kings of Judah, rather than of David himself; David would have been buried in the ancient City of David.) In any event, the room of the Last Supper is also probably the same one in which Jesus appeared to his disciples after his resurrection, and where the Holy Spirit descended at Pentecost.

There is a possibility that this is indeed the correct location for the upper room. According to Epiphanius, a fourth century bishop who lived in Palestine for at least 20 years, several first century buildings had survived into the time of Hadrian (A.D. 135). Among these was the small Christian church. If the original Christian community continued to meet in the upper room, then it is likely that Epiphanius' small church was at that location.

When this church was rebuilt on a larger scale in the late fourth century, it was called the Upper Church of the Apostles; a century later it was known as the Mother of Zion Church. A small apse in the "Tomb of David" is all that remains of this church, since it was burned during the Persian invasion in A.D. 614. Finally, a mosaic floor in Madaba, Jordan (about A.D. 600) includes a depiction of the church in just this area of Jerusalem.

THE HOUSE OF CAIAPHAS

The house of Caiaphas (who was the high priest during the trial of Jesus) is no doubt in the area of other luxurious homes on the Western Hill. The location has traditionally been identified with the Church of St. Peter in Gallicantu (St. Peter of the Cock Crow), but there is very little evidence to support this. It was once assumed that a unique set of weights found at the site was a special kind used only at the Temple, and which the high priest might have in his home. We now know, however, that there was considerable variety in the types of weights, so these were not necessarily unique to the Temple. A more likely identification of the house of Caiaphas is that of the Herodian Mansion.

WHAT CAN WE LEARN FROM JESUS TIME IN JERUSALEM?

A TEMPORARY DEATH

A young Jewish man was showing his Christian friends from America around Jerusalem. Wishing to be helpful, he took them to the Church of the Holy Sepulchre. Then he heard that there was another place, called the Garden Tomb, which may be the correct location. Striving to not be negligent in his duty, he took them to the Garden Tomb as well.

While waiting for his friends there he exclaimed, "I don't get it. The Catholics have Jesus buried over there. The Protestants seem to think he is buried here."

A Christian overheard the remark and said, "Oh, he isn't buried here either."

Thinking there was yet another place, he turned in astonishment to hear more. "You mean he isn't here?"

The stranger replied, "No! He is risen from the dead."

We too must remember that the former occupant of the grave is more important than the grave itself. Jesus is no longer dead, but is alive and well and seated at the right-hand of the thrown of God. Remember this story:

> *But on the first day of the week, at early dawn, they went to the tomb,*
> *taking the spices they had prepared. And they found the stone rolled*
> *away from the tomb, but when they went in they did not find the body*
> *of the Lord Jesus. While they were perplexed about this, behold, two*
> *men stood by them in dazzling apparel. And as they were frightened*
> *and bowed their faces to the ground, the men said to them, "Why*
> *do you seek the living among the dead? He is not here, but has risen.*
> *Remember how he told you, while he was still in Galilee, that the Son*
> *of Man must be delivered into the hands of sinful men and be crucified*
> *and on the third day rise."*
>
> LUKE 24:1-7

With the exception of Peter and John (John 20:1-10), no one else seems to have visited the tomb after the resurrection. What was important was the fact that it was empty: for Jesus, the grave was only a temporary residence.

This tomb, however, played an important part in the gospel story. Jesus was buried in a particular kind of tomb, the knowledge of which helps us understand the prophecy of Isaiah:

> *He was assigned a grave with the wicked, and with the rich in*
> *his death, though he had done no violence, nor was any deceit in*
> *his mouth.*
>
> ISAIAH 53:9

Jesus' burial in the tomb of a rich man, Joseph of Arimathea, was an aspect of what the Messiah would go through. Let us examine more closely the tomb of Jesus.

Then he took [Jesus' body] down, wrapped it in linen cloth and placed
it in a tomb cut in the rock, one in which no one had yet been laid.

LUKE 23:50-53

A tomb in which no one had been laid: what other kind of tomb is there? Who would think of reusing a tomb? Since Old Testament times, people had been buried in family tombs. A cave would be hewn out of the rock, with ledges prepared to receive the wrapped body of the deceased.

When people died, they would quite literally be "gathered to their fathers"; a family tomb would serve quite well for hundreds of years. But since Joseph's hometown was too far from Jerusalem to be buried before sunset on the day of his demise, he dug a new one close by.

But this was no ordinary tomb: it had a rolling stone.

Most tombs were closed with a stone plug, but a rolling stone tomb was sealed with a large stone disk which rolled back and forth in a slot. Rolling stone tombs were so rare that the only examples we have belong to royalty. For example, when Queen Helene of Adiabene converted to Judaism, she came to Jerusalem to live. Her elaborate tomb complex (erroneously known as the Tomb of the Kings, north of Damascus Gate near the American Colony Hotel) is an excellent example of this kind of tomb. The family of Herod was also buried in a rolling stone tomb (behind the King David Hotel). What these tombs have in common, besides their construction, is the fact that they belonged to very wealthy people. Joseph must have been quite rich. By the very tomb described in the Gospels, we know that Jesus was associated with the rich in his death.

What is most important about the tomb, however, is that it was empty. His grave was temporary, just like his death. His accommodations, however, were first-class.

Because of the Resurrection our deaths arc temporary, too. There is no reason to fear death, no reason to dread the grave. The One who stepped from his new grave long ago will also call us from our temporary resting place:

in a moment, in the twinkling of an eye, at the last trumpet. For
the trumpet will sound, and the dead will be raised imperishable,
and we shall be changed. For this perishable body must put on the
imperishable, and this mortal body must put on immortality. When
the perishable puts on the imperishable, and the mortal puts on

immortality, then shall come to pass the saying that is written: "Death is swallowed up in victory." "O death, where is your victory? O death, where is your sting?"

1 CORINTHIANS 15:52-55

TEMPLE MOUNT
THE MEETING PLACE OF GOD

How lovely is your dwelling place, O LORD Almighty!

PSALM 84:1

BACKGROUND, ARCHAEOLOGY AND SIGNIFICANCE:

BACKGROUND

Perhaps the most easily recognized part of Jerusalem, the Temple Mount is located within the walls on the eastern side of the Old City. The site of Solomon's temple and the later temple built by Herod the Great is now an enormous stone platform for the Dome of the Rock and the El Aksa Mosque.

The graceful arched entryways at the perimeters of the platform frame the views of the Mount of Olives to the east, and the densely populated Old City to the west. Jews come here to pray at the Western Wall. Muslims come to pray at the Dome of the Rock and the El Aksa Mosque. Israeli soldiers and the Arab Temple Mount Police protect what may be the most revered spot on the face of the earth.

THE ARCHAEOLOGY OF THE TEMPLE MOUNT

The temples built by Solomon and Herod shared more than a location. They shared a similar fate. Both temples were completely destroyed in war. Nothing remains of the original buildings of which were said, "He who has never seen the temple has never seen a beautiful thing in his life."

The Western Wall is only a portion of the retaining wall on which the temple stood. The rest of the wall was hidden by a millennium of building activity.

In 1987, archaeologists were finally able to reveal all 1,500 feet of the wall. Entering through a passageway from the plaza in front of the Western Wall, you proceed along a road that runs along the front of the wall. Some stones are up to 10 feet high and nearly 45 feet long.

The great temples built by Solomon and Herod were both destroyed.

Parts of the platform and staircases are the only remnants of these temples.

The platform now houses the Dome of the Rock and the El Aksa Mosque .

Solomon's temple was destroyed in the Babylonian invasion of 586 B.C.

Herod the Great's temple was destroyed by the Romans in A.D. 70.

REFERENCES

2 Samuel 7:1-17; 24:16-25

1 Kings 5 - 6; 7 - 10

2 Kings 11-12; 22:1 - 23:25; 25:8-17

Psalm 26:8; 42:4; 48:1-3; 84; 87; 134

Isaiah 6

Jeremiah 7:1-15

Ezra 3 -6

Ezekiel 8 10; 40 - 44

Matthew 21:12-16; 21:23 24:2; 27:3-10,51

Mark 11:11, 15-19; 11:27 13:2

Luke 1:5-25, 2:22-38,41-50; 4:9-12; 19:45 - 21:6

John 2:13-22; 5:14; 7:14 8:59; 10:22-39

Acts 3:1-4:3; 21:27 22:30

In 1984, work on the tunnel was stopped when the excavators found a passage leading to corridors below the temple area itself. After three years of negotiations, Muslim and Jewish religious authorities agreed not to excavate below the Temple Mount.

The temple platform, built by Herod beginning in 19 B.C., was estimated to be twice the size of Solomon's temple, which was built nine hundred years earlier. In order to enlarge the temple area, Herod built extensions on the earlier wall and added new southern and western walls. The seam between Herod's addition and the original wall may be seen on the eastern side of the Temple Mount, south of the Golden Gate.

According to Josephus, it took Herod's workmen eight years just to quarry and shape the stones for the walls, and a thousand wagons were used to move them from the quarry to the temple area. Herod's stones have a distinctive margin around the edges; you will notice many of them in the Western Wall. You will also see some very weathered stones without the margin; these may be stones that were reused from Solomon's temple platform.

In some places, the retaining walls rose 100 feet above the level of the streets below. On the southeastern corner of the platform, the walls continued below the level of the street to the bedrock. The platform was built partly on bedrock and partly on supporting arches, which are sometimes erroneously called "Solomon's Stables."

The main public access to the platform was from the south, through double and triple gates, called the Huldah Gate. These handled enormous crowds during festivals, perhaps up to 150,000 people at a time. The triple-arched gate was the entrance and the double-arched gate served as the exit. These gates have been filled in, but you can still see their outlines in the walls near the well-preserved steps of the monumental southern staircase.

The triple-arched entryway on the southeast led to a tunnel that brought the worshipers up to the platform area. On the platform, they would be surrounded with columned porches. To leave the platform, they would exit the western Huldah Gate, and down a staircase four times larger than the entry staircase, since everyone would leave at the same time when the ceremony was over. The steps of this wider staircase are well preserved, and this is one of the few places we know that Jesus walked.

In the large courtyard area on top of the Temple Mount, there was a wall of stone latticework five feet high between the Court of the Gentiles and the holy area. There was an inscription on the partition in Greek and Latin forbidding gentile trespassers to go beyond it.

Nothing else remains of the temple itself. The white limestone columns and the gold gilding of their capitals are all gone. Ten years of work went into the main buildings, and seventy-three years were spent on improvements. Only the retaining wall and the staircases remain.

THE TEMPLE MOUNT IN THE OLD TESTAMENT

Solomon built the First Temple on the threshing floor that his father David purchased from Araunah the Jebusite (2 Samuel 24:18-25). The site was hallowed as the place where God stayed the hand of Abraham as he was about to sacrifice his son Isaac on Mount Moriah (2 Chronicles 3:1), and where God stopped the plague against the Israelites (2 Samuel 24:15-18).

The temple was the center of worship for Israel's united kingdom. When the kingdom divided after Solomon's death, the temple served the kingdom of Judah until its destruction by the Babylonians in 586 BC. The returning exiles under Ezra rebuilt the temple, but on a far more modest scale.

THE TEMPLE MOUNT IN THE NEW TESTAMENT

Like other firstborn Jewish babies, Jesus was brought to the temple by Mary and Joseph in order to redeem him according to the Law:

> The LORD said to Moses, "Consecrate to me every firstborn male.
> The first offspring of every womb among the Israelites belongs to me,
> whether man or animal."
>
> EXODUS 13:1-2

While in the temple, both Simeon and Anna prophesied about the future of the baby they were holding. As he grew up, Jesus would have been brought to the temple three times a year for the pilgrimage festivals. Luke records that after Passover, Jesus stayed behind in Jerusalem as his parents started home. Mary and Joseph found him in the temple courtyards, listening and asking questions of the teachers. Even at this early age, Jesus demonstrated an awareness of his identity:

> *"Why were you searching for me?" he asked. "Didn't you know I had*
> *to be in my Father's house?"*

LUKE 2:49

As an adult, Jesus continued to come to Jerusalem for the feasts, to teach and to heal. Jesus used his opportunities to teach on the temple grounds:

> *As he looked up, Jesus saw the rich putting their gifts into the temple*
> *treasury. He also saw a poor widow put in two very small copper coins.*
> *"I tell you the truth," he said, "this poor widow has put in more than*
> *all the others. All these people gave their gifts out of their wealth; but*
> *she out of her poverty put in all she had to live on."*

LUKE 21:1-4

Jesus also asserted his divinity in the colonnaded porches known as the Portico of Solomon. Here in the temple courts, the scribes and Pharisees brought a woman caught in adultery and asked Jesus for his verdict. He forgave her, telling her accusers that anyone without sin could throw the first stone (John 8:1-11). Jesus also chased out the moneychangers here at the Temple Mount (Matthew 21:12 13; Mark 11:15-17; Luke 19:45-46; John 2:14-16).

In the book of Acts, the disciples continued to come to the temple to worship and teach, just as Jesus had done before them. At the gate on the eastern side of the temple platform, Peter healed the lame man (Acts 3:1-10). During Paul's last visit to the temple, a riot ensued when he was charged with bringing Gentiles into the area where only Jews were allowed:

> *When the seven days were nearly over, some Jews from the province*
> *of Asia saw Paul at the temple. They stirred up the whole crowd and*
> *seized him, shouting, "Men of Israel, help us! This is the man who*
> *teaches all men everywhere against our people and our law and this*
> *place. And besides, he has brought Greeks into the temple area and*

defiled this holy place." (They had previously seen Trophimus the
Ephesian in the city with Paul and assumed that Paul had brought him
into the temple area.)

When Jesus' disciples commented on the beauty of the Temple, Jesus told them:

"As for what you see here, the time will come when not one stone will
be left on another; every one of them will be thrown down."

LUKE 21:5-6

His prophecy was fulfilled when the Romans conquered Jerusalem and destroyed the temple in A.D. 70.

WHAT CAN WE LEARN FROM THE TEMPLE MOUNT?

UNRESTRICTED ACCESS TO THE MOST HOLY PLACE

Access to the temple was restricted. According an inscription on the partitioning wall, non-Jews could not enter under penalty of death. They were only allowed on the colonnaded porches.

Even Jews could not access the whole temple. Jewish women could enter beyond the Court of the Women, where chests were placed to receive gifts for the cost of the services. It was here that the widow deposited her two coins (Mark 12:41-44).

Jewish men could enter the Court of Israel, a raised area closer to the temple itself. Once a year at the Feast of Tabernacles, Jewish men were allowed into the Priests' Court. Still, they remained more than thirty feet away from the porch of the Temple itself. Further inside, the Holy Place was off limits to everyone but priests.

The most holy area of the temple, called the Holy of Holies, was where the presence of the Lord dwelt in a special way. Although Jews knew that God was everywhere, there was a special way in which his presence was enthroned above the mercy seat, the top of the Ark of the Covenant. Once a year, on the Day of Atonement, the high priest would enter the Holy of Holies with the blood from the slain sacrifice, and sprinkle it on the mercy seat.

185

The inner sections of the temple served as a reminder of the absolute holiness of God. His presence was not to be treated lightly. Violations of the sacredness of the Most Holy Place were punishable by death. It was meant to be forbidding, yet intense in beauty. It was holy, yet belonged to all God's people. It was inaccessible to most, yet provided atonement for all.

While the temple was overlaid with gold, our access to God was purchased at a much higher cost: the life of his Son. And though the temple was built with restricted access to God, we now have unrestricted access to the Father. The temple was eventually destroyed, but the Priesthood of Christ is enduring.

God is a father who invites his children to come to Him. The invitation is open. The barriers have been removed.

> *"Let us then approach the throne of grace with confidence, so that we may receive mercy and find grace to help us in our time of need."*
>
> HEBREWS 4:16

JEWISH QUARTER
A RELIGIOUS PLACE OF GREAT IMPORTANCE

They restored Jerusalem as far as the Broad Wall.

NEHEMIAH 3:8

BACKGROUND, ARCHAEOLOGY AND SIGNIFICANCE:

FIRST IMPRESSIONS

The Jewish Quarter fits the biblical description of Jerusalem as a city "compacted together" (Psalm 122:3). New buildings of honey- colored limestone are being built around small courtyards, flower boxes in the windows with their red and pink geraniums cascading down the sides of the balconies. The boutiques in the fashionable Cardo are perhaps not much different than their predecessors in this main street of Jerusalem, for this area was always the more wealthy and luxurious place to live, the "up-town" address of high priests and officials.

Between 1948 and 1967, the Jewish Quarter was almost completely destroyed. After the Six-Day War in 1967, extensive excavations were performed in the area before the Quarter was rebuilt. Therefore, below the streets are the remains of the houses destroyed in the numerous conquests of the city as far back as the time of Jeremiah in 586 B.C. Small "windows", revealing such remains, have been left in various places along the streets, giving you glimpses into the city's past.

THE JEWISH QUARTER IN THE OLD TESTAMENT

This area of Jerusalem on what is called the Western Hill was not part of the original City of David. As the population expanded in the centuries, after King David made Jerusalem the capital of the kingdom, additional room for housing were found on the Western Hill. The shallow Tyropaean Valley separates this hill from the Temple Mount and the City of David. This suburb was known as the Mishneh, Hebrew for the "second area". Anticipating the attack of the Assyrians, King Hezekiah constructed an additional

QUICK FACTS

This was the section of Jerusalem where the Religious Leaders lived in Jesus time

Some parts of this Quarter have been found to date back as far as 586 B.C.

In this part of the city we can see remains of the Cardo, the Broad Wall and houses from the Herodian Period, including "The Burnt House"

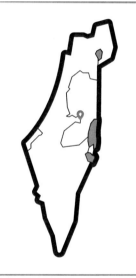

REFERENCES

2 Kings 22:14

2 Chronicles 34:22

Nehemiah 3:8; 11:9

Isaiah 22:10

Jeremiah 39:1-3, 8-10

Zephaniah 1:10-11

Matthew 26:57-75

Mark 14:53 - 15:1

Luke 22:54-71

John 11 :47-53; 18:12-27

Acts 4:5-22; 5:21-41; 6:12-7:56; 22:30; 23:10

189

wall, the "Broad Wall", to include part of what is now the Jewish Quarter. Huldah, the prophetess, lived in the Mishneh (2 Kings 22:14); the officials of King Josiah sought her out so that she would ask the Lord about the fate of the nation.

This section of the city felt the wrath of the Babylonian invasion:

And Jeremiah remained in the court of the guard until the day that Jerusalem was taken.

> *In the ninth year of Zedekiah king of Judah, in the tenth month,*
> *Nebuchadnezzar king of Babylon and all his army came against*
> *Jerusalem and besieged it. In the eleventh year of Zedekiah, in the*
> *fourth month, on the ninth day of the month, a breach was made in*
> *the city.*
>
> JEREMIAH 38:28-39:2

Jeremiah's description of the conquest goes on to imply that the initial breach of the city's defenses occurred in the area of the Middle Gate, identified with the tower and gate found north of the Broad Wall. After the return of the exiles, Nehemiah supervised the repair of the wall, which included an area up to the Broad Wall.

THE JEWISH QUARTER IN THE NEW TESTAMENT

In the New Testament, the area on the Western Hill was the wealthy district of Jerusalem. From Josephus' description of structures destroyed in this area during the Roman conquest, this appears to be the location of a number of the buildings associated with the trials of Jesus. The houses of Caiaphas the high priest and his father-in-law Annas (the previous high priest) were in the Jewish Quarter; there also was a special entrance that led from the Jewish Quarter across the Tyropaean Valley to the Temple Mount. Jesus was questioned first at the home of Annas; it in Annas' courtyard that Peter denied that he knew Jesus three times. After being beaten and mocked at Caiaphas' house, Jesus was taken over to the Sanhedrin for trial.

The Sanhedrin met at the Chamber of Hewn Stone to try Jesus on the charge of blasphemy; it too was located in this Quarter. From there Jesus was taken to Pilate, who sent Jesus to Herod Antipas for questioning. Depending upon where Herod Antipas was staying, this interrogation may have been occurred in the palace of the Hasmoneans (the former royal family of Intertestamental times), located west of the Temple Mount in the Jewish Quarter.

The Sanhedrin was the scene of several incidents in the book of Acts as well. Peter and John were brought here after healing a lame man at a gate of the Temple. Eventually, all the apostles were arrested. After a miraculous escape from prison, they appeared before the Sanhedrin, where the high priest warned them:

> And when they had brought them, they set them before the council.
> And the high priest questioned them, saying, "We strictly charged you
> not to teach in this name, yet here you have filled Jerusalem with your
> teaching, and you intend to bring this man's blood upon us." But Peter
> and the apostles answered, "We must obey God rather than men."
>
> ACTS 5:27-29

Stephen was the next believer to appear before the Sanhedrin. At the end of his defense he was taken out of the city and stoned to death (Acts 6:12-7:60). Towards the end of Acts, Paul was taken before the Sanhedrin as well. Although Paul was the last one recorded in scripture to have been tried by the Sanhedrin, Josephus records that James, the half-brother of Jesus, was also tried; the biblical record, however, is silent about his death.

THE ARCHAEOLOGY OF THE JEWISH QUARTER

The excavation of the Jewish Quarter allowed a large area of the ancient city to be studied before new residential construction began. Numerous houses, dating to the eighth century B.C., add to our understanding of everyday life for the people of the suburbs. Some of these may have belonged to refugees from the Northern Kingdom, for the city seems to have quadrupled in size at the end of the 700's (Samaria fell in 722 B.C.). The finds from the houses included the usual household pottery, as well as clay figurines. These images included fertility figurines, used to insure the fertility of humans, animals, and crops. The popularity of such idols sheds light on the prophets' calls for repentance.

Called in the Bible the Mishneh or Second District, the quarter was enclosed by the wall built by King Hezekiah in the late 700s B.C. One stretch of the wall was particularly thick (over 22 feet) and should probably be identified with the Broad Wall mentioned in Isaiah 22:10 and Nehemiah 3:8. Isaiah describes what is today known as the state's right of eminent domain:

You counted the buildings in Jerusalem and tore down houses to
strengthen the wall.

ISAIAH 22:10

The course of the wall has been exposed for a length of over 200 feet. Most of what remains of the Broad Wall is only the lower foundations, although in one area the wall is still over 10 feet high.

At the base of a nearby tower, two types of arrowheads were found. One type was an iron arrowhead typical of Israelite forces; the other was a bronze type called "Scythian", used by foreign mercenary troops employed by the Babylonians and others. The heavy ash deposits and arrowheads here seem to indicate that the battle against the Babylonian army was intense in this area.

THE HERODIAN MANSION
(Wohl Archaeological Museum)

The most impressive building ever excavated in Jerusalem is called the Herodian Mansion (named after the period in which it was built, not the owner). This two-story, two thousand square foot mansion included pools, ritual baths, and cisterns. The walls had frescoes of geometric and faux marble designs. Careful Torah observance is indicated by the meticulous avoidance of representational art, as well as numerous ritual bathing installations.

The furniture, pottery, glassware, and other finds suggest wealth, leading the excavators to suggest that this might be the home of one of the high priests. The mansion's proximity to the Burnt House, with its inscription linking it with the high priestly family, would strengthen the identification as either the house of Annas or Caiaphas. We know from Josephus that Ananias, a later high priest (A.D. 47-55), lived on the Western Hill near the Hasmonean Palace, so the general location of this family of high priests would be correct.

"THE BURNT HOUSE" MUSEUM
(Kathros' House)

A house found near the Herodian Mansion had been destroyed in the heavy conflagration of the Roman destruction of A.D. 70. More testimony of the destruction was revealed when the bones of a severed forearm were found in the kitchen. Among the unusual finds in this house was a stone mold for casting coins and a workshop for manufacturing something for the temple, possibly incense or spices. The owner's name, found on an inscription, was "Bar Kathros" (son of Kathros). The name is known from the Talmud as the member of a high priestly family known for corruption, greed, and violence.

The Byzantine Cardo

The most important street in any Roman city was the cardo maximus, like a Main Street of today. Portrayed in detail on the Madaba Map in Jordan, the Cardo of Jerusalem was a colonnaded street running north and south with a column at the end. The street corresponding to the colonnaded cardo has been found, providing a key to the locations of other buildings on the map. A section of the street has been reconstructed to give visitors an understanding of the city as the Romans rebuilt it.

WHAT CAN WE LEARN FROM THE JEWISH QUARTER?

HULDAH THE PROPHETESS AND ALL THE KING'S MEN

One of the most remarkable people that ever lived in this quarter was Huldah the prophetess. While we often associate the title of "prophet" with one who foretells the future, most of the prophetic statements in the Bible are there to proclaim a current truth, "to tell it like it is" to individuals and the nation.

Before the time of King Josiah in the late 600's B.C., the worship of God was in a sad state. For one thing, the Temple was filled with religious articles for other gods, as well as living quarters for male cult prostitutes. Devotion to the Lord was not exactly a high priority.

Yes, there was the Temple of the Lord that Solomon had built nearly four centuries earlier. Even though the Assyrians had conquered those idol-worshiping Samaritans to the north, God had miraculously spared Jerusalem when Josiah's great- grandfather Hezekiah was king. But no one seemed to know where a copy of the Bible was, much less what it said.

It was at this time that the Book of the Law (the first five books of the Bible) was found in a dusty corner of the Temple. When it was read to the king, he discovered that the Bible carried bad news for him and his country:

> *When the king heard the words of the Book of the Law, he tore his*
> *clothes. And the king commanded Hilkiah the priest, and Ahikam*

the son of Shaphan, and Achbor the son of Micaiah, and Shaphan

the secretary, and Asaiah the king's servant, saying, "Go, inquire

of the Lord for me, and for the people, and for all Judah, concerning

the words of this book that has been found. For great is the wrath

of the Lord that is kindled against us, because our fathers have not

obeyed the words of this book, to do according to all that is written

concerning us."

2 KINGS 22:11-13

Something had to be done. The situation had persisted for a very long time, and the king knew that something drastic would happen if they didn't act soon. But what were they to do? At the time, none of the king's officials or spiritual advisers happened to be on speaking terms with the Almighty.

So they found someone who was:

So Hilkiah the priest, and Ahikam, and Achbor, and Shaphan, and

Asaiah went to Huldah the prophetess, the wife of Shallum the son

of Tikvah, son of Harhas, keeper of the wardrobe (now she lived in

Jerusalem in the Second Quarter), and they talked with her. And she

said to them, "Thus says the Lord, the God of Israel: 'Tell the man who

sent you to me, Thus says the Lord, Behold, I will bring disaster upon

this place and upon its inhabitants, all the words of the book that the

king of Judah has read.

2 KINGS 22:14-16

The priests and royal officials lived in the City of David and the precincts of the royal palace; Huldah lived in the Second Quarter. The quarter had not yet become an area for the wealthy and important; that stage would wait until after the return from the Babylonian exile.

Instead, it was the houses in Huldah's quarter that had been confiscated to strengthen the city walls. It was this area of town that served as housing for the war refugees from Samaria to the north. Although Huldah did not live in the "right area," people did know to go to her for direction, for a word from God.

How do people know who is on speaking terms with God? In this case, having the right religious title was not the answer. Neither was living in the right part of town. The Bible does not say how the officials knew that Huldah was the right person to talk to-but somehow, they knew.

It should be our goal to have such a close relationship with God that others around us know we can talk to God or on behalf of God. In 1 Peter we are told to be ready to give an account for the hope that is within us (1 Peter 3:15). The only way that we will be able to do so is if we are living in such a way that our relationship with God is evident in our actions. According to Jesus, the world should be able to know that about us as well:

You are the light of the world. A city set on a hill cannot be hidden.
Neither do people light a lamp and put it under a bowl. Instead they
put it on its stand, and it gives light to everyone in the house.In the
same way, let your light shine before men, that they may see your good
deeds and praise your Father in heaven.

MATTHEW 5:14-16

JERICHO

THE CITY OF PALMS

At the sound of the trumpet, when the people gave a loud shout,
the wall collapsed...

JOSHUA 6:20

BACKGROUND, ARCHAEOLOGY AND SIGNIFICANCE

THE HISTORY OF JERICHO

Archaeological evidence of bones, stone vessels, and flint tools date as far back as 9000 B.C. The site continued to be inhabited sporadically for centuries, with occasional gaps in occupation. However, the dates of the walls and the times of abandonment have been heavily contested.

While the Bible states that Joshua conquered Jericho, some scholars have asserted that Jericho was not inhabited at that time in history. Recent studies, however, have shown that this earlier analysis may have disregarded evidence that would support the biblical account.

The city was inhabited by Israelites from the ninth century until the Babylonian exile. There are no remains on the tell later than the Babylonian destruction in 586 B.C. The people who resettled the area after the return apparently moved to the site of the modern city of Jericho.

The region remained strategically and economically important during the intertestamental period. During that time, the focus of the city moved about a mile further south, where the Wadi Qelt emerges onto the plain of the Jordan Valley. The Hasmonean royal family eventually built an extensive palace and agricultural estate here.

During the Roman period, Jericho became a regional capital. Herod took control of the area when the Romans granted him kingship. He began his building projects in Jericho in about 35 B.C., only to have Mark Antony give the area away as a special gift to Cleopatra. After the deaths of Antony and Cleopatra, Caesar Augustus returned the region to Herod, along with its royal palaces and estates.

REFERENCES

Numbers 22:1, 26:3, 63, 31:12, 33:48-50, 34:15, 35:1, 36:13

Deuteronomy 32:49, 34:1, 3

Joshua 2, 3:16, 4:13, 19, 5:10, 13, 6, 7:2, 8:2, 9:3, 10:1, 28-30, 12:9, 13:32, 16:1,7, 18:12, 21, 20:8, 24:11

2 Samuel 10:5

2 Kings 2:1-18, 25:5

2 Chronicles 28:15

Nehemiah 3:2, 7:36

1 Kings 16:34

1 Chronicles 6:78, 19:5

Ezra 2:34

Jeremiah 39:5, 52:8

Matthew 20:29-34

Mark 10:46-52

Luke 10:25-37, 18:35 - 19:27

Hebrews 11:30-31

Over the next twenty years he constructed two additional palaces with elaborate gardens and pools. Herod died here in 4 B.C. After his death, a former slave named Simon burned down the palace. Herod's son Archelaus rebuilt it, but on a diminished scale.

The city remained prosperous during Jesus' lifetime, but the Romans destroyed it during the First Jewish Revolt. It was rebuilt during the reign of Hadrian and remained a Jewish city well into the sixth century.

THE ARCHAEOLOGY OF OLD TESTAMENT JERICHO

The earliest archaeological remains in Jericho have been dated to about 9000 B.C. Remains of hut floors date to a few hundred years later when the village expanded around the area of the spring. Around 7000 B.C. the villagers worked together to construct a large fortification wall, with a large tower next to it. The tower was more than 27 feet in diameter at its base and is preserved to a height of 25 feet. A staircase in the center provides access to the top of the tower. The houses built at this time had rounded foundations and are called "beehive" houses by archaeologists.

In the next period of occupation (6000-5500 B.C.) the plan of the houses changed, as did the forms of worship. Human skulls were found covered in plaster and modeled to resemble living heads. They had shells for eyes and paint for the skin and hair. These may indicate some kind of ancestor worship or cult practice. The plastered skulls may be seen in the Rockefeller Museum in Jerusalem or in the British Museum in London.

Excavations of Jericho's tombs have added valuable information about everyday life at the time that Abraham lived among the Canaanites. Furniture, baskets, platters of fruit and meat, jewelry, boxes of carved bone and other items have been well preserved for almost four thousand years because of the dry climate.

The city suffered a violent destruction in about 1600 B.C., probably at the hands of an Egyptian pharaoh of the powerful 18th Dynasty.

A collapsed double wall found by archaeologist John Garstang may correspond to Joshua's conquest of the city. The remains of Jericho from the ninth to the sixth centuries B.C. are very fragmentary, mostly because of erosion. However, evidence from tombs shows that the city continued to be inhabited until the Babylonian invasion.

After the exile, there are biblical references to people returning to Jericho under Zerubbabel (Ezra 2:34) and some of these people assisted in the repair of Jerusalem's walls under Nehemiah (Nehemiah 7:36). Archaeological evidence for this period in Jericho is very scanty, perhaps because the population was spread out, living in the cultivated areas rather than on the tell.

THE ARCHAEOLOGY OF NEW TESTAMENT JERICHO

Hasmonean king John Hyrcanus I (134-104 B.C.) built a palace and a large royal estate here. He also built a water channel from the Wadi Qelt springs. Subsequent Hasmonean rulers added villas, pools, and additional gardens to the original palace; remains of these buildings have been excavated on the northern side of the riverbed.

Herod the Great built three different palaces in Jericho, eventually connecting them together. His first palace was on the south side of the riverbed, across from the palace built by his in-laws, the Hasmoneans. The plan of Herod's palace was much like Roman villas found at Pompeii, with rooms built around a central courtyard.

The walls of the buildings feature an unusual type of construction that Herod the Great imported from Rome. The construction is called opus reticulatum and was fashionable in Rome when Herod visited there. This style consists of pie-shaped bricks, square on the outer end and laid in a diagonal pattern.

In about 25 B.C. Herod built a second palace using the same general plan as the first. It was located on the north side of the riverbed, on the ruins of the Hasmonean palace, which had been destroyed by an earthquake. Ten years later, he built his third palace in Jericho. This was by far his most spectacular. It included buildings on both sides of the riverbed with a bridge between them. This palace boasted extensive gardens, several pools, and a Roman bath complex.

A hippodrome, theatre, and amphitheater were discovered between the old Jericho site and Herod's palace. This entertainment complex (of which only the foundations survive) included a racetrack, which could have been used for horse and chariot racing.

An enormous cemetery at the bottom of the mountain slope was used during the first centuries B.C. and A.D. Its size indicates a large population in Jericho during that period. The wealth of the royal families attracted people who could be employed in the estates, the palace, entertainment complex, and other industries.

Jericho was deserted when the Roman army came to put down the revolt in A.D. 66. After the revolt, a Roman garrison was stationed in Jericho. The Roman road was paved and marked with milestones. The route may still be followed today along the southern side of Wadi Qelt. On the same side of the wadi is the aqueduct that brought water to Herod's palaces and gardens.

JERICHO IN THE BIBLE

When the trumpets sounded, the people shouted, and at the sound of the trumpet, when the people gave a loud shout, the wall collapsed; so every man charged straight in, and they wok the city.

JOSHUA 6:20

Jericho was the first city that Joshua and the Israelites conquered after crossing the Jordan River. Two spies had entered the city to assess its defenses. Rahab the prostitute hid them, and in return they promised to spare her and her family when the city was taken.

When the walls of Jericho fell, the Israelites thoroughly destroyed the city and set fire to it. As the first city of their conquest, it was considered an offering to God and whoever rebuilt the city would be cursed. Even though it was in the region allotted to the tribe of Benjamin, it was not occupied.

Eventually, in the ninth century B.C., Hiel of Bethel reoccupied and built a wall around the city. The description in 1 Kings 16:34 suggests that his sons were offered as a foundation offering, a practice forbidden in the Bible.

In Ahab's time, Hiel of Bethel rebuilt Jericho. He laid its foundations
at the cost of his firstborn son Abiram, and he set up its gates at the
cost of his youngest son Segub, in accordance with the word of the
LORD spoken by Joshua son of Nun.

JOSHUA 16:34

The city's location on a fault zone causes the springs to change location and sometimes to become bitter or fresh. During the time of Elisha, the spring became undrinkable and made the land unproductive. Elisha threw salt into the water and prayed, purifying the water.

The last mention of Jericho before the exile comes when the pursuing Babylonians captured Zedekiah, the last king of Judah, on the plains of Jericho.

In the New Testament, Jesus passed through Jericho on his final journey to Jerusalem. While in Jericho, he healed two blind men (though Mark and Luke only record one, Bartimaeus). At this time, Jesus was also the guest of the tax collector Zacchaeus (Luke 19:1-10). On this same occasion, Jesus told the parable of the ten minas (Luke 19:12-27).

WHAT CAN WE LEARN FROM JERICHO?

A MAN OF NOBLE BIRTH

"A man of noble birth went to a distant country to have himself
appointed king and then to return. So he called ten of his servants and
gave them ten minas. 'Put this money to work,' he said, 'until I come
back.' But his subjects hated him and sent a delegation after him to
say, 'We don't want this man to be our king...'"

LUKE 19:12-14

According to Luke's gospel, Jesus told the parable of the ten minas (or talents) in Jericho just before entering Jerusalem for the last time. The context of Jericho is significant. The story of a king going to a distant country to receive a kingdom would have resonated clearly. King Herod traveled to Rome, where the Roman senate declared him King of the Jews.

Jesus may have wanted to emphasize the differences between the kingdom of God and the kingdoms of men – especially that of Herod. Herod's cruelty would have been familiar to the people of Jericho.

However, like a human king, God rewards his stewards according to their ability to invest the resources he has given them. In this parable, we have both parallels and contrasts with the realm of human leadership. Joshua and others had to steward their gifting and call in Jericho, in the face of fear and opposition. We too must do what God calls us to do no matter the opposition. There will be times our fear paralyzes us, but God will enable us to be able to make the wise decision and obey in righteousness.

We can be confident however, that we will meet a good king in the last day.

> *"His master replied, 'Well done, good and faithful servant! You have been faithful with a few things; I will put you in charge of many things. Come and share your master's happiness!'"*

MATTHEW 25:23

THE JUDAEAN WILDERNESS

GOD'S TESTING GROUND

...like streams of water in the desert and the shadow of a great
rock in a thirsty land.

ISAIAH 32:2

BACKGROUND, ARCHAEOLOGY AND SIGNIFICANCE

BACKGROUND

Desolate crags and dusty, infertile soil epitomize the Judaean wilderness. The steep descent to the Dead Sea from the Judaean hills consists of deep canyons cutting through a rocky wasteland, both foreboding and awesome in its beauty. Limited rainfall and blistering temperatures make the wilderness nearly inhospitable. The Wilderness of Judaea is not to be confused with the desert of Sinai, where the Israelites wandered for 40 years.

THE HISTORY OF THE JUDAEAN WILDERNESS

Because of its location east of the Judaean hill country, the wilderness acted as a natural buffer zone and defense against enemies from the east. There were east-west routes through the wilderness from Jerusalem to Jericho and from Bethlehem to En Gedi.

In response to threats from the east, forts were built to protect these roads. One of these outposts was at En Gedi, on the shores of the Dead Sea. A fortified town was built there in the seventh century B.C. There are also remains of an earlier settlement, perhaps that of David.

Although the wilderness was not conducive to permanent settlement, it played an important role in harboring fugitives, outcasts, and hermits. The largest population ever to live in the wilderness was a group of Christian monks during the Byzantine period.

The largest monastery in the wilderness is that of Mar Saba. It was founded in A.D. 483 and is still in operation. Its founder, Saint Sabas, came to Israel from Cappadocia (Turkey) and at the age of 30 established himself in a cave in the Judean Wilderness. After several others joined him,

The Judaean wilderness provided a natural barrier and defense from the east.

This is where David escaped from Saul on multiple occasions.

This wilderness was the setting for John the Baptist's ministry.

Jesus faced Satan's temptation in the Judaean Wilderness.

REFERENCES

Joshua 2:16-23: 15:61; 16:1; 18:12

Judges 1:16

1 Samuel 17:28; 22: 1-5: 23: 14 - 26:25

2 Samuel 15:23-16:14; 17:1-22 1

Chronicles 12:8-18

2 Chronicles 20: 1-28

Psalm 63

Isaiah 16: I: 35: 1.6: 40:3-5

Jeremiah 4: 11: 5:6; 9:2,10,12; 12:12; 22:6: 23:10: 31:2

Lamentations 4:19; 5:9

Matthew 3:1-4: 11; 11:7-19

Luke 1:80; 3:2-20: 4:13: 7:24-35; 10:30-37

Psalm 63

Mark 1:2-1

they established a monastery on the cliffs of the Kidron Valley.

Christian ascetics came to live in the area's many caves, joining for worship but otherwise remaining separate. The monastery became so populous that Sabas had to build another one nearby in A.D. 493. It is said the narrow canyons in the wilderness echoed with the singing of these hermits.

THE WILDERNESS LANDSCAPE

The Judaean Wilderness is often referred to in the Bible simply as "wilderness." Its Hebrew name, Yeshimon, means "devastation." The wilderness is about 15 miles across at its widest east-west point and about 35 miles long, north to south. The eastern border of the wilderness is the Dead Sea, where cliffs drop 1,300 feet to the Jordan Valley floor.

The western boundary is less distinct, as the wilderness ascends to meet the limestone Mount of Olives. Because of the steepness of the twisted canyons, even the downhill journey from Jerusalem to Jericho is a six-hour walk.

Despite the obvious appearance of barren, rocky hillsides, a spring rain can result in brief blooms of wildflowers and grass. The water held in the bottom of some canyons attracts shepherds. Careful water conservation and collection allows nomadic sheep and goat herders to reside in the wilderness east of Bethlehem.

THE JUDAEAN WILDERNESS IN THE BIBLE

The uninviting nature of the wilderness made it an excellent place for refuge. The Israelite spies hid here after escaping from Jericho (Joshua 2:16, 23). There were at least two times that David went to the wilderness to hide from Saul. In 1 Samuel 22:4 David hid from Saul in a place called

Masada, which means, "The Stronghold" in Hebrew. It's possible that this is the same Masada that Herod fortified during his reign.

During the reign of King Jehoshaphat of Judah (873-849 B.C.), a Moabite-Ammonite coalition invaded the kingdom of Judah by way of En Gedi (2 Chronicles 20:1-28). As a response to Jehoshaphat's prayer, God arranged for his enemies to slaughter each other east of Tekoa.

In the New Testament, the Judean Wilderness provided the backdrop for the ministry of John the Baptist. It also set the scene for the parable of the Good Samaritan (Luke 10:30-37). Away from the watchful eye of the Roman soldiers, thieves were known to attack travelers along the wilderness roads.

It was also here in the Judaean wilderness that Satan tempted Jesus (Matthew 4:1-11 and Mark 1:12-13). Jesus would later pass through the wilderness on a number of occasions. For example, he stopped at Jericho on his last journey to Jerusalem (Luke 19:1- 11).

WHAT CAN WE LEARN FROM THE JUDAEAN WILDERNESS?

THE WILDERNESS—GOD'S TESTING GROUND

For we do not have a high priest who is unable to sympathize with our weaknesses, but we have one who has been tempted in every way, just as we are—yet was without sin.

HEBREWS 4:15

We often think of temptation as an abundance of pleasures and things that attract our senses but the Bible provides a different picture of temptation. In the wilderness, the bare necessities of life are not readily available. Desert plants bloom briefly and infrequently, and the occasional deer scratches out a meager existence on the margins.

The test of the wilderness comes in how content we are with God's provision, no matter how little it may seem. In the wilderness of Sinai, the Israelites were stripped of the provisions they were accustomed to. There was no Nile River for water, no vegetables to farm, no fowl, no fish, and no flour for bread. There was nothing but God.

Like the Israelites, Jesus walked along the brink of physical survival. After going without food, company or comfort for 40 days, he was tempted. It was not in the midst of plenty, but in the midst of desolation that the

Son of God was tested. Would he be satisfied with God's provision and promises? Would he be satisfied with his mission, though it led to suffering and death? Where most of us would break in complete misery, Jesus proved that he was content with God.

Take your stand in the wilderness with Jesus. Is God sufficient? Is His grace and forgiveness more than enough? Here, where there is nothing but His presence, meditate upon His provision in your life.

See, I am doing a new thing! Now it springs up; do you not perceive it? The wild animals honor me, the jackals and the owls, because I provide water in the desert and streams in the wasteland, to give drink to my people, my chosen, the people I formed for myself that they may proclaim my praise.

ISAIAH 43:19-21

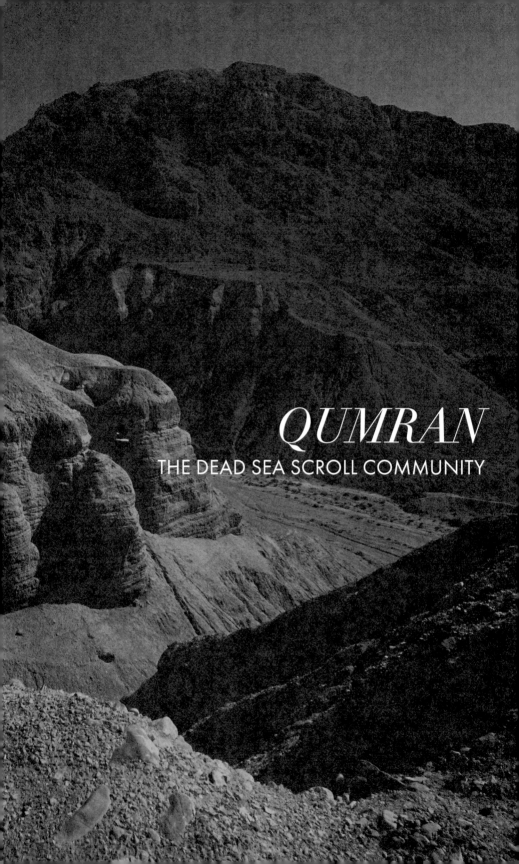

QUMRAN

THE DEAD SEA SCROLL COMMUNITY

BACKGROUND, ARCHAEOLOGY AND SIGNIFICANCE

BACKGROUND

The surroundings of Qumran could not be more stark and hostile. The sulphurous fumes from nearby hot springs, the glassy shroud over the Dead Sea, scorching temperatures in the summer, and imposing cliffs all combine to make this an inhospitable place to live.

It is understandable why early archaeological excavations overlooked such an unremarkable site. It was not until the discovery of the Dead Sea Scrolls that attention was turned toward the village site itself.

THE HISTORY OF QUMRAN

The area of Qumran had been occupied since Old Testament times. One of the buildings dates to the eighth century B.C., possibly as a military installation. The oldest arrow (shaft and arrowhead) ever discovered has been dated between 700 and 600 B.C. The site was subsequently abandoned for about 400 years.

A Jewish group opposed to the religious establishment in Jerusalem resettled Qumran in about 150 BC. According to texts discovered at Qumran, a priest called the "Teacher of Righteousness" came into conflict with an opponent called the "Wicked Priest" and withdrew to form his own community apart from the "congregation of traitors."

The Hasmonean king Jonathan usurped the high priesthood in 152 B.C., so it is possible that he is the one referred to as the "Wicked Priest." The settlers at Qumran were probably a group that Josephus refers to as Essenes. Although Essenes eventually lived in several cities including Jerusalem, Qumran was perhaps their first safe haven during the reign of the Hasmonean kings.

The small community received an influx of people during the reign of Alexander Jannaeus around 100 B.C. It was this king who killed over 56,000 Jews during his reign, crucifying 800 of them. According to Josephus, he had women and children massacred while he watched and feasted with his concubines. Again, religious dissidents fled to Qumran.

Communal life at Qumran ended in A.D. 68 during the First Jewish Revolt, when Roman troops captured the site. In anticipation of that event, the inhabitants carefully hid their writings in jars and put them in nearby caves. The site functioned for a short time as a Roman fort between A.D. 69 and 74. The destruction of the community (or the fact that they fled elsewhere) was the end of Qumran.

THE ARCHAEOLOGY OF QUMRAN

The earliest archaeological remains at Qumran date to the time of Isaiah, about 700 B.C. At that time, a rectangular building was constructed. This was possibly a small fort that included a row of small rooms along a courtyard, and a cistern. The building was partially destroyed during the Babylonian invasion of 587-586 B.C. and remained unoccupied until the religious community moved to Qumran around 150 B.C.

Foundation stones from the former building were reused to construct the heart of the settlement, to which the community added over the next two centuries. One round cistern to the west belonged to the original building, but the Qumran community added two more reservoirs and ritual baths. Water channels collected runoff from rainwater and fed the reservoirs.

The influx of people into the community around 100 B.C. required an additional water supply. The increased demand was met by building a dam across the wadi to catch water from flash floods during the winter. Four large cisterns and two more ritual baths were also added.

The buildings of the community eventually took the form you see today. Two of the most important rooms are the scriptorium and the assembly hall. The scriptorium was a long, narrow room that scribes used to copy the bible and other documents.

In the upper story of this room, archaeologists found inkwells containing dry ink, writing pallets, benches, and tables. These clues indicate that at least some of the scrolls found in the nearby caves were written here.

A ritual bath south of the scriptorium would have been used by members of the community before meals. Food and dishes were stored in a nearby pantry and a kitchen was used to prepare meals. Judging by the remains, the diet of the community consisted of lamb, mutton, goat, veal, beef, legumes, and vegetables.

The southeastern area contained a large ritual bath and a potter's workshop. The jars that held the Dead Sea Scrolls were made here. There are no signs of rooms for sleeping, and it's possible that members slept in tents, temporary structures or nearby caves. The caves show evidence of occupation during this period. The earthquake in 31 B.C. destroyed much of the site, including over a thousand dishes and other items in the pantry.

The site was reoccupied in about 4 B.C., apparently by the same group that left 27 years earlier. They repaired damaged buildings but left rooms that could not easily be repaired. The courtyards were roofed over to give additional shelter. According to coins found in the rubble, the village was finally destroyed during the third year of the First Revolt, A.D. 68-69. The Roman soldiers who destroyed Qumran (as evidenced by numerous Roman arrowheads) occupied it until the fortress at Masada was finally taken in A.D. 74.

The cemetery was located 50 yards east of the buildings and contained over 1,100 tombs. Very few people in any of the tombs had ever reached their forties.

THE CAVES AND THE DEAD SEA SCROLLS

In 1947, bedouin shepherd boys from the Ta'amireh tribe were looking for lost sheep among the hills west of Qumran. One boy threw a stone into a cave (now called Cave one) and heard a cracking sound. The boys returned the next day with adults to see what was in the cave.

After removing several jars, they were disappointed to see that they only contained scrolls. They took them to a Bethlehem antiquities dealer to see what price they could fetch. They were eventually shown to several scholars, who verified that they were ancient manuscripts of the Bible, a thousand years older than any biblical manuscript then known to exist.

E.L. Sukenik of Hebrew University in Jerusalem realized their importance. He borrowed enough money and even mortgaged his own house to make the dangerous trip to Bethlehem to purchase three of the seven scrolls. The next day, the United Nations vote creating the state of Israel meant that Sukenik would not be able to return to Bethlehem to obtain the remaining scrolls, since they were now in the territory belonging to Jordan. The four remaining scrolls were later purchased in New York from the Assyrian Orthodox Church for $250,000.

The hunt began to find where the scrolls came from. In 1949, a search of the area around Qumran resulted in the discovery of more caves, containing jars with manuscripts hidden inside. The documents were incredibly well preserved because of the dry climate. In all, eleven caves contained manuscripts. Cave four alone held 516 documents. Unfortunately, Roman soldiers had ripped them into more than 15,000 fragments, presumably when the site was taken during the First Jewish Revolt.

The Dead Sea Scrolls consist of more than 800 documents in all. Some are copies of books of the Old Testament. Every book in the Old Testament is represented with the exception of Esther. Other scrolls contain later Jewish writings known as the Apocrypha and Pseudepigrapha. A large number of scrolls contain information about rules of the community and biblical commentaries that reflect their beliefs. There are also letters, hymns, prayers, and other writings. The Manual of Discipline, for example, describes the rules for participation in the community at Qumran and provides a window into their life and beliefs.

Other scrolls include the Copper Scroll, found on a shelf carved into the back of Cave Three. It claims to describe the places where the treasure from the Temple in Jerusalem was buried. Another manuscript, the Psalm Scroll, was found in 1967 after the Six-Day War in the home of the antiquities dealer who first handled the scrolls. The Psalm Scroll is preserved to a length of 28 feet, although part of the scroll had deteriorated in the relative dampness of Bethlehem. Another important manuscript, the Temple Scroll, contains detailed instructions for the eventual rebuilding of the Temple in Jerusalem.

The finding of the Dead Sea Scrolls is important for several reasons. First, we now have multiple copies of books of the Old Testament. Second, they are more ancient than any previously known copies. Because of this, they have vindicated the accuracy of the traditional text of the Hebrew Bible, with only very minor differences. The scrolls have also given us a more complete view of Judaism at the time of Christ. There were a much greater variety of Jewish sects than the Pharisees and Sadducees that appear in the New Testament.

RELIGIOUS BELIEFS OF THE QUMRAN COMMUNITY

One of the central beliefs of the community was that they were the elect people of God, reserved as the remnant of Israel until the time that God would restore his rule to the land. Several of their writings explain the conditions for admittance into the community, the requirements for living there, and penalties for misconduct. The community was highly organized with strict discipline.

Ritual purity was extremely important to the community. Their writings concerning daily regulations and penalties for purity violations indicate a very strong desire to keep the community from uncleanliness. The purified Jerusalem that the community envisioned, the nearest latrine was to be three thousand cubits from the city; since the limit for walking on the Sabbath was two thousand cubits, it is clear that there were to be no visits to the latrine on that day.

The topic of the purification of the priesthood brings the discussion to the origins of the Qumran sect and possibly their identity. The texts of the community protest that the current priesthood was illegitimate, as it was not occupied by a descendant of Zadok, a priest from the Old Testament. It is for this reason that, even though the community was concerned about ritual matters, they despised the religious establishment in Jerusalem. As far as the Qumran community was concerned, the illegitimacy of the priesthood made the sacrifices at the Temple unacceptable to God.

QUMRAN, THE BIBLE, AND CHRISTIANITY

The fact that the Qumran community existed at the same time as the beginning of Christianity has led some scholars to attempt to discover a link between Qumran and Christianity. There are certainly parallels between the Qumran community and the early Christian movement. However, most of those who have emphasized the similarities between the Qumran community and the Christian church have failed to take into account their differences.

These differences are themselves enough to discount any positive connection between the two groups. For example, while the Qumran texts stress the central importance of ritual purity, the New Testament presents Jesus as relatively unconcerned with regulations regarding cleanliness and uncleanliness. Jesus was criticized for associating with sinners, healing on the Sabbath, and breaking other rules that were important to the Qumran sect.

More importantly, the goals of Jesus and the goals of the Qumran community were, if not incompatible, at least in no way related.

Furthermore, the claim by some that Christianity really began as a Jewish sect is as astounding as the claim that the United States had its roots in the English colonies. It can safely be stated that Christianity and the Qumran community had some things in common. They shared the Jewish worldview, the Jewish Scriptures, and the Jewish God. Any parallels between the two movements can be attributed to their common origin in Judaism.

WHAT CAN WE LEARN FROM QUMRAN?

SALT AND LIGHT BY THE DEAD SEA?

> *"You have heard that it was said, 'You shall love your neighbor and hate your enemy.' But I tell you: Love your enemies and pray for those who persecute you..."*
>
> MATTHEW 5:43

In this verse, Jesus seems to imply that the Jews taught hatred for their enemies. But no such sentiment had ever been expressed in the Old Testament, the Talmud or any other Jewish scripture. Jewish scholars had long been puzzled by this assertion by Jesus.

Now we know. In the War Scroll, one of the writings of the Qumran community, it is stated: "Love your friends; hate your enemies." Jesus was quoting the Essenes at Qumran, not the Pharisees or a mainstream Jewish group. The teaching of God in the Bible was clear.

> *"Do not seek revenge or bear a grudge against one of your people, but love your neighbor as yourself. I am the LORD."*
>
> LEVITICUS 19:18

How was it possible that the Qumran community, a group so devoted to copying the scriptures and writing commentaries, hymns, and prayers based on their study, missed the point of Leviticus 19:18? Perhaps their withdrawal from the world and into the desert demanded a mindset of loving friends and hating enemies. The covenant community at Qumran apparently excused their hatred of outsiders by narrowing their definition of "neighbor."

This belief of the Qumran community provides interesting background for Jesus' conversation with an expert in the Law recorded in Luke 10:25 37, the parable of the Good Samaritan. The expert had asked Jesus, "Who is my neighbor?" The story is a familiar one. A man was robbed and beaten on the road, and a priest and a Levite refuse to stop and help.

Meanwhile, a hated Samaritan renders assistance and even gives beyond what was reasonably expected. Jesus told the expert in the Law, "Go and do likewise." The definition of "neighbor" is left unanswered, because there are no limitations on acts of kindness.

> *But I say to you, Love your enemies and pray for those who persecute you, so that you may be sons of your Father who is in heaven. For he makes his sun rise on the evil and on the good, and sends rain on the just and on the unjust. For if you love those who love you, what reward do you have? Do not even the tax collectors do the same? And if you greet only your brothers, what more are you doing than others? Do not even the Gentiles do the same? You therefore must be perfect, as your heavenly Father is perfect.*

MATTHEW 5:44-48

Jesus opposed the human tendency to separate with people of like mind and to care for only those who care for us. We have Jesus' example as well as his command.

> *And the scribes of the Pharisees, when they saw that he was eating with sinners and tax collectors, said to his disciples, "Why does he eat with tax collectors and sinners?" And when Jesus heard it, he said to them, "Those who are well have no need of a physician, but those who are sick. I came not to call the righteous, but sinners."*

MARK 2:16-17

EN GEDI

THE HIDDEN PLACE

And David went up from there and lived in the strongholds of
En Gedi.

1 SAMUEL 23:29

BACKGROUND, ARCHAEOLOGY AND SIGNIFICANCE

BACKGROUND

En Gedi is one of the most delightful surprises in Israel. It is a sparkling oasis, hidden in a canyon cut through the barren cliffs of the Judaean wilderness. En Gedi means "spring of the kid." The water cascades from the rock, down a series of waterfalls into shallow pools. Water flows from the pools down the canyon, where vegetation lines the stream bed.

The coolness of the water is a stark contrast with the heat of the wilderness. The spring and stream draw animals to their banks, including gazelles, deer, wild goats, and badgers. The area is part of a nature preserve that protects the two parallel canyons of Nahal David and Nahal Arugot, both of which enjoy the presence of waterfalls and pools.

THE HISTORY OF EN GEDI

The remains of a Canaanite temple dating to about 3500 B.C. sit on a cliff above Nahal David. Since there are no remains of houses in the area, it's assumed nomadic people who brought their sheep to water used this temple. The spring was used as a place of refuge for centuries but it does not appear to have been permanently settled until the end of the seventh century B.C., when an Israelite fortress was built here. The Babylonians destroyed the fort before the destruction of Jerusalem in 586 B.C., and the site was abandoned for about a century. The area was later reoccupied by Jewish exiles returning from Babylon.

The oasis became important during the Roman period, known for its date palms and balsam. At the beginning of the First Revolt in A.D. 66 AD, the town was raided by the Sicarii, the Jewish group that fostered the rebellion. Seven hundred

QUICK FACTS

David sought refuge here when hiding from Saul.

An Israelite fortress was built here in the seventh century B.C.

Remains of an earlier Canaanite temple date to about 3500 B.C.

Copper-age artifacts from the Canaanite temple were found in a nearby cave.

REFERENCES

Genesis 14:7

1 Samuel 23:29; 24:1

Song of Solomon 1:14

Joshua 15:62

2 Chronicles 20:2

Ezekiel 47:10

people were killed here. The site was resettled at the end of the first century. It continued as a Jewish town as late as the sixth century A.D., when a synagogue was built here.

EN GEDI IN THE BIBLE

En Gedi is first mentioned in the Bible as part of the story of Abraham's victory against the four Mesopotamian kings (Genesis 14:7). En Gedi is known in this account, as well as in 2 Chronicles 20:2, as Hazazon-Tamar.

En Gedi was allotted to the tribe of Judah, and was used by shepherds such as David when there was nothing for the sheep to eat in the hills. David also used En Gedi as a refuge when hiding from Saul. David and his men hid in a cave here when Saul paused briefly in his pursuit:

> *[Saul] came to the sheep pens along the way; a cave was there, and Saul went in to relieve himself. David and his men were far back in the cave. The men said, "This is the day the LORD spoke of when he said to you, 'I will give your enemy into your hands for you to deal with as you wish.'" Then David crept up unnoticed and cut off a corner of Saul's robe.*
>
> 1 SAMUEL 24:3-4

En Gedi is also where the combined forces of Moab and Ammon were camped when King Jehoshaphat (869-853 B.C.) learned of the invasion. When he prayed for protection, the invaders were destroyed by the time he arrived.

THE ARCHAEOLOGY OF EN GEDI

Excavations were conducted in 1949 and from 1961 to 1965. A copper-age temple, dating to about 3500 B.C., was discovered. Numerous copper objects were found in a nearby cave, including crowns, scepters, and mace heads. It appears that these were carefully hidden before the temple was abandoned. The objects from this cave are on display in the Israel Museum.

The town of En Gedi was located at a site called Tel Goren, not far from the spring. The Israelites built a series of fortresses here. Permanent settlement seems to have begun in the late seventh century BC. Some historians believe the ovens and pottery were part of a perfume production industry. The town was destroyed in the Babylonian invasion and resettled on a larger scale after the exile.

The walls of a Roman bath provide evidence that En Gedi was resettled after the First Revolt. The Jewish community continued well into the sixth century A.D. A mosaic inscription on the synagogue floor says, "Peace on Israel."

WHAT CAN WE LEARN FROM EN GEDI?

THE HIDING PLACE AS PREPARATION

You are my hiding place; you will protect me from trouble and surround
me with songs of deliverance.

PSALM 32:7

David spent several years hiding from King Saul. As a result, the "hiding place" is one of David's images for God. David could feel hidden and protected in the canyon. He had water in abundance, vegetation to eat and animals for meat. With such lavish provision all around, it is easy to forget that this hidden paradise is actually in the midst of a wasteland.

We see a similar example of God's protection when Elijah's life was in danger.

And the word of the Lord came to him: "Depart from here and turn
eastward and hide yourself by the brook Cherith, which is east of the
Jordan. You shall drink from the brook, and I have commanded the
ravens to feed you there." So he went and did according to the word
of the Lord. He went and lived by the brook Cherith that is east of the
Jordan. And the ravens brought him bread and meat in the morning,
and bread and meat in the evening, and he drank from the brook.

1 KINGS 17:2-6

There are times when God's people need rest. At times, we need a hiding place for refreshment and renewal. But both David and Elijah eventually left their places of refuge. Although God's protection and provision were permanent, the isolation of a hiding place was not. Both men had important work to do.

Elijah's time of hiding lasted three years, and he went on to challenge the prophets of Baal on Mount Carmel. David eventually left his hiding place to become King of Israel.

In periods of hardship, God sometimes surprises us with an oasis like En Gedi, a place of physical, spiritual, and emotional refreshment. But eventually, there comes a time to move away from these temporary shelters. We have a call minster to others, to fight spiritual battles, and perhaps lead other hurting people to a needed oasis.

MASADA

STRONGHOLD ON THE DEAD SEA

So strong had the fortress's defenses against enemy been made
both by nature and by human effort.

JOSEPHUS, JEWISH WAR 7.8

BACKGROUND, ARCHAEOLOGY AND SIGNIFICANCE

BACKGROUND

Along the south shore of the Dead Sea, visitors will notice a particular cliff that stands out from the rest. A monolith of rock rises separately from the cliffs around it, forming a natural castle with a dry moat. Imposing and isolated, this is Masada.

It would take a feat of engineering to build on top of this plateau. Rising 1,460 feet above the Dead Sea, moving supplies and water to the top was not an easy task.

The view from the Northern Palace offers a vast view of the surroundings, making it clear why this was an ideal place for a fort. The ruins are characteristic of Herod the Great, who combined his architectural flair and political paranoia in the construction of this desert hideaway.

THE HISTORY OF MASADA

The mountain was used as a refuge in Old Testament times, from the time of David to about 600 B.C. The first period of substantial building took place during the reign of Jonathan, the Hasmonean ruler (161-143 B.C.). Likewise, Herod the Great saw the potential of this location. He added to the existing Hasmonean structure and built an additional palace on the northern end of the plateau. He also built an elaborate water-supply system to enable the fortress to withstand a long siege.

During the First Revolt against Rome, the rebel forces under Menachen Ben-Yehuda overpowered the Roman garrison at Masada in A.D. 66. When Jerusalem was destroyed in A.D. 70, leaders of the revolt fled to Masada. They lived there for two years before the Roman procurator Flavius Silva began the siege in earnest.

QUICK FACTS

Masada was used as a fortress from the time of David.

Herod the Great added elaborate palaces and fortifications.

It was the site of a great siege during the First Revolt against Rome.

It was largely forgotten after the first millennium A.D. and rediscovered in 1842.

REFERENCES

1 Samuel 23:14, 29; 24:22

2 Samuel 22:3

Psalm 9:9; 59:9; 62:2

Silva built a wall around the mountain to cut off all supplies. On the first day of Passover in 73, the defenders realized that their situation was hopeless. They chose to burn their fortress and commit suicide rather than to fall into the hands of the Romans.

The site was inhabited again in the fourth and fifth centuries by Christian monks who considered Masada an ideal retreat. They built a small church there. The Crusaders used the site briefly as a fortress in A.D.1000.

MASADA IN THE OLD TESTAMENT

Masada means "stronghold" in Hebrew. The word appears in several verses of the Old Testament, but one reference is likely to refer specifically to the place called Masada today. When David fled from Saul, David took his parents to Moab for their safety. Then he took refuge in what is called the "Masada" or stronghold (1 Samuel 22:4). Located about ten miles from the oasis of En Gedi, Masada is the best natural fortress in the area. Archaeological remains confirm that it was used in the tenth century B.C., the time of David.

THE SIEGE OF MASADA

Those living in Masada from the beginning of the revolt in A.D. 66 didn't come under siege until A.D. 72. In the meantime, they altered the palaces and storerooms to accommodate refugee families. They were able to grow crops on top of the mountain and food was rationed among the families.

When the Roman general Silva finally marched against Masada, he brought an estimated 10,000 to 15,000 troops to besiege the fortress held by only 967 people. Silva first built camps behind an encircling wall. This cut off all supplies and aid to the defenders.

Using Jewish captives, he then constructed a ramp from the eastern side up to the walls. A barrage of arrows and stones from catapults kept the defenders from interfering. Finally, with the ramp complete, multi-story siege engines (like towers on wheels) were rolled up the ramp to weaken the walls. When the defenders tried to set the siege engines on fire, the winds turned the fire back toward the defenders.

On the first day of Passover in A.D. 73, the garrison realized their situation was hopeless. The speech of their commander Eleazar, the substance of which is recorded in Josephus, encouraged the people to take their own lives rather than to fall into the hands of the Romans to be tortured, killed, or enslaved.

They chose to burn their possessions, except for food, to prove to the Romans that they had not been starved. Ten men were selected by lot to kill the others. One of the ten then killed the other nine and himself. However, two women and five children had hidden in the conduits that brought the water into cisterns. They alone lived to tell what had happened.

THE ARCHAEOLOGY OF MASADA

Israeli archaeologist Yigael Yadin led the excavation of Masada from 1963 to 1965. It was an enormous undertaking. No other location in Israel has yielded so many remains of every aspect of life, which can be dated so precisely. The excavations have helped us appreciate Herod's grandiose architectural plans. His palaces, storerooms, fortification walls, bathing complexes, and water installations have all been revealed.

During the Hasmonean period, a complex of four mansions was built on the western side of the mountain. The largest had a courtyard at the center with two reception rooms, a large hall (possibly a throne room), and a small bath house. Herod used these buildings to house his family when he fled the Parthians in 40 B.C. This complex became the nucleus of Herod's Western Palace.

Herod added storehouses for provisions and a water supply system. He had twelve large cisterns quarried out of the rock in the northwest side of the cliff. They were filled with water from the wadis around Masada. Herod also built two or three large cisterns filled by rainwater. There was still enough water to fill the swimming pool in the south, as well as all the bathing complexes.

Herod's most ambitious project at Masada was Northern Palace, built on three terraces. The lowest terrace is the best preserved. Its reception hall contained frescoes that imitated marble walls. The middle terrace included a colonnaded round building. The main living quarters were located in the upper terrace, again with colonnaded verandas.

To strengthen the natural defenses of the mountain, Herod added a double wall over 4,500 feet in length around the perimeter. Thirty towers were placed at intervals on the wall. Two gates defended the only two paths to the top, the snake path on the east (where hikers and the tram passengers enter today) and a path on the west, which was later covered up by the Roman siege ramp.

The most poignant discoveries come from the last defenders in A.D. 73, attesting to their deeply religious life. Fourteen fragments of scrolls have been found. Some are of books of the Bible, including Genesis, Leviticus, Deuteronomy, Ezekiel, and Psalms. Others are from the Apocryphal books, Ben-Sirah and Jubilees.

A synagogue and ritual bath located on the western side of the plateau served some of their religious needs. Two fragments of the Torah were found in the back room of this synagogue underneath the floor. They even had a beth-midrash or "house of study" with stone benches along the sides and in the center of a large hall.

Among the more than 700 pieces of broken pottery, were "coupons" for the rations of the priests, marked "priest's tithe." Some vessels were inscribed with the word "holy" and had ritual purposes, for the priests and Levites who conducted religious services.

Near the inner gate of the Northern Palace, ten pottery fragments were found with names inscribed on them, one of which, "Ben- Yair", the family name of Eleazar, is mentioned by Josephus as the leader of the group. These broken pieces of pottery may be the lots that were used to choose the ten who would kill the others.

The skeletons of the 960 people who died have never been found. The Romans or their Jewish prisoners of war may have gathered the bones and buried them. Evidence of the fire set by the defenders is concentrated in several rooms. Charred remains of furniture and other combustibles are covered with piles of ash. This discovery substantiates Josephus' account that they gathered their belongings in one place and set them on fire.

THE MODERN HISTORY OF MASADA

Masada faded from the memory of people living in the land after the first millennium A.D. An English painter named Tipping, who was working on an illustrated edition of Josephus' Jewish War, rediscovered the fortress in 1842. A short time later, renewed interest in the site prompted American, French, and German expeditions to excavate the site over the next 80 years.

Masada has since become an important symbol for the modern state of Israel. The mountain symbolizes courage, heroism, and a legacy of repeated assaults against Jews. In the 1940s it became a pilgrimage site for groups fighting for a Jewish homeland. "Masada shall not fall again" became the slogan of these movements.

After the War of Independence, the Israeli flag was hoisted on Masada. For a time, the recruits of the Armor Corps and officers of the Israel Defense Forces were sworn in at Masada. It is also a traditional place of pilgrimage during Hanukkah in December, a holiday that commemorates the Maccabean heroes who attained victory against impossible odds.

WHAT CAN WE LEARN FROM MASADA?

THE MODERN HISTORY OF MASADA
THE FORTRESS THAT CAN NEVER BE TAKEN

Masada was thought to be an impregnable fortress. Herod had made every effort to ensure that no one would ever conquer it. Yet Masada is now famous for its ultimate defeat.

King David understood the natural defenses of rocky ramparts like Masada. He frequently used the words "rock" and "fortress" as pictures of safety and escape.

> *The Lord is my rock and my fortress and my deliverer, my God, my rock, in whom I take refuge, my shield, and the horn of my salvation, my stronghold.*
>
> PSALM 18:2

> *For who is God, but the Lord? And who is a rock, except our God?*
>
> PSALM 18:31

> *He made my feet like the feet of a deer and set me secure on the heights.*
>
> PSALM 18:33

> *The Lord lives, and blessed be my rock, and exalted be the God of my salvation*
>
> PSALM 18:46

Remembering his protection at Masada, David wrote this song to God. While the rocks served a physical purpose, the Lord was his refuge and protection. Ultimately, David knew his safety did not come from a fortress. Even Masada could be taken by a determined enemy. David's confidence was found in God.

In our own lives, we tend to hold "fortresses" that we regard as invulnerable. We can become falsely reliant on ourselves far too easily. We may quickly become over-confident in our money, or become wrapped up in our status or possessions. We can easily take relationships for granted.

Real security is found on the true rock, God himself. Like a truly unconquerable fortress, God's promises support us.

> *In you, O Lord, do I take refuge; let me never be put to shame; in your righteousness deliver me! Incline your ear to me; rescue me speedily! Be a rock of refuge for me, a strong fortress to save me! For you are my rock and my fortress; and for your name's sake you lead me and guide me;*
>
> PSALM 31:1-3

As you stand on the deserted fortress of Masada, spend time reflecting on God as your source of strength. Christ teaches us that He is the rock upon which we must build our lives. To rely on anything else is temporary and foolish.

> *"Everyone then who hears these words of mine and does them will be like a wise man who built his house on the rock. And the rain fell, and the floods came, and the winds blew and beat on that house, but it did not fall, because it had been founded on the rock. And everyone who hears these words of mine and does not do them will be like a foolish man who built his house on the sand. And the rain fell, and the floods came, and the winds blew and beat against that house, and it fell, and great was the fall of it."*
>
> MATTHEW 7:24-27

THE DEAD SEA

THE BITTER END OF THE JORDAN

It is a scorching, arid, repulsive solitude.... It makes one think of funerals and death.

MARK TWAIN, "THE INNOCENTS ABROAD"

BACKGROUND, ARCHAEOLOGY AND SIGNIFICANCE

BACKGROUND

The Dead Sea creates a landscape of eerie desolation. The searing hot temperatures, white salt and bleached chalky soil make the ground appear baked and blistered. A haze hovers over the sea from rapid evaporation and the surface of the water appears deathly still. The Hebrew name, Yam Hammavet, or "Sea of Death" is apt for this body of water. It the Bible, it is usually referred to as the Salt Sea.

THE DEAD SEA AND ITS LANDSCAPE

The Dead Sea is the lowest place on dry ground at 1,294 feet below sea level. It sits in the Jordan Valley between the hills of Moab to the east and the Judaean Wilderness to the west. The Jordan River enters the sea from the north, and the area south of the sea is known as the Sodom Plain. The sea is about 48 miles long and 10 miles wide. It is 1,500 feet deep at the northern end, and becomes increasingly shallow toward the south.

There are a number of springs around the Dead Sea's perimeter. Some produce fresh water, while others emit brackish water and sulfurous gases. The two largest fresh water springs on the west are at En Gedi and Ein Fashkha. On the eastern side, four main streams flow into the sea. The areas around these streams are surprisingly fertile, an indication that the five biblical cities that existed nearby could have been more prosperous than appearances might suggest.

The Dead Sea has no outlet. This factor, combined with the numerous mineral hot springs and high salt content, makes the water extremely dense with solids. The water evaporates and leaves the mineral content behind. The chemi-

QUICK FACTS

At 1,294 feet below sea level, The Dead Sea is the world's lowest point on land.

Its salt and mineral content is too high to support any fish or plant life.

Sodom, Gomorrah and the five "cities of the plain" were near the Dead Sea.

REFERENCES

Genesis 13:10-13; 14:1-12, 17; 18:16-19:29

Numbers 34:3, 12

Deuteronomy 3:17; 4:49

Joshua 3:16; 12:3; 15:2, 5; 18:19

Ezekiel 47:8-11, 18

cals present in the water include salt, potash, magnesium, calcium chlorides and bromide. Today, both Israelis and Jordanians operate chemical plants on the shores of the Dead Sea to extract minerals.

These are used primarily for fertilizers and agricultural use. Cosmetic companies use these some of these minerals as well.

The sea has a salt concentration of over 25 percent, making it impossible for fish or plants to survive. It is also impossible for a person to sink in the thick, high-buoyancy water. Several beaches offer swimming and mud baths. The Jordan River is now diverted for agricultural purposes, causing the southern part of the sea to slowly dry up, and increasing the salt content.

THE DEAD SEA IN THE BIBLE

The Dead Sea is known by several names in the Bible including the Salt Sea, the sea of the Aravah, and the Eastern Sea. The campaign of the four kings of Mesopotamia against the five "cities of the plain" in Genesis 14 indicates more fertility and human presence around the Dead Sea than is visible today.

This is the area that Lot, Abraham's nephew, chose because it had better pasture for his flocks than the Judaean hill country. God destroyed two of these cities, Sodom and Gomorrah, by raining down burning sulfur. It is possible that the igniting of sulfur (brimstone) and bitumen during an earth quake could have produced the effect described in the Bible.

For most of Israel's history, the Dead Sea was the boundary between Judah on the west and Moab and Ammon on the cast (2 Chronicles 20:1-30). However, the sea was not an insurmountable barrier to invasion. It was possible to ford the sea by going across a peninsula of land protruding from the eastern shore to within two miles of the western shore. Masada would have been used to guard this eastern entrance into Judaea. There are also traces of a Roman road crossing this outcrop of land.

Zephaniah mentions the salty marsh at the southern end of the Dead Sea:

"Therefore, as I live," declares the Lord of hosts, the God of Israel,
"Moab shall become like Sodom, and the Ammonites like Gomorrah,
a land possessed by nettles and salt pits, and a waste forever. The
remnant of my people shall plunder them, and the survivors of my
nation shall possess them."

ZEPHANIAH 2:9

Throughout scripture, the destruction of Sodom and Gomorrah is used as a symbol of God's judgment on immorality. In Ezekiel 47, the healing of the waters of the Dead Sea represent God's mercy and restoration of what had been devastated.

While there are no explicit references to the Dead Sea in the New Testament, we know from Josephus that John the Baptist was beheaded in Herod's palace called Machaerus. This palace was located on the cliffs overlooking the eastern shore of the Dead Sea.

WHAT CAN WE LEARN FROM THE DEAD SEA?

A TRANSFORMATION TO THE SEA OF LIFE

The Dead Sea is a place of desolation and lifelessness. It is a place with abundant water but no fish. There is moisture, but little plant life. Its waters are toxic to living creatures.

Now imagine that the Dead Sea was brought to life. Imagine that its waters were made clean and that it teemed with fish. Imagine the valley irrigated for agriculture and teeming with wildlife. Imagine the Dead Sea transformed and renamed, the Sea of Life.

God showed the prophet Ezekiel a scene like this, as a picture of God's renewing power:

> Then he brought me back to the door of the temple, and behold, water was issuing from below the threshold of the temple toward the east (for the temple faced east). The water was flowing down from below the south end of the threshold of the temple, south of the altar...and it was a river that I could not pass through, for the water had risen. It was deep enough to swim in, a river that could not be passed through. And he said to me, "Son of man, have you seen this?"
>
> Then he led me back to the bank of the river. As I went back, I saw on the bank of the river very many trees on the one side and on the other. And he said to me, "This water flows toward the eastern region and goes down into the Arabah, and enters the sea; when the water flows into the sea, the water will become fresh. And wherever the river goes, every living creature that swarms will live, and there will be very many fish. For this water goes there, that the waters of the sea may become fresh; so everything will live where the river goes. Fishermen will stand beside the sea. From Engedi to Eneglaim it will be a place for the

spreading of nets. Its fish will be of very many kinds, like the fish of the
Great Sea.

EZEKIEL 47:1, 5-10

That scene becomes even more meaningful when we remember that Ezekiel wrote it during Israel's captivity in Babylon. The Temple had been destroyed, the people were taken away and Jerusalem was left in ruins. Yet God gave a message of hope through Ezekiel, communicated in this picture of the Dead Sea transformed.

There may be people or situations in our lives that we quickly judge as hopeless cases. But to God, there arc no hopeless cases. No one is beyond the reach of his love. There is no one who cannot be renewed. All of us can be forgiven. In the resurrection of His Son, God demonstrated His power to transform death into life. We can have hope where there is hopelessness, joy where there is sorrow and wholeness even as we are broken. Nothing is out of the reach of God's renewing hand.

Look at the Dead Sea and imagine the Sea of Life. Use that image to see hope in every hopeless situation. God can transform any life and he can bring beauty from the ashes.

"So there is nothing-nothing too sunken, too useless, too doomed –
but by the grace of God it may be redeemed, lifted, and made rich
with life."

GEORGE ADAM SMITH,
"THE HISTORICAL GEOGRAPHY OF THE HOLY LAND"